encounters

encounters

AUTHENTIC EXPERIENCES OF GOD

JOHN WOOLMER

MONARCH
BOOKS

Oxford, UK & Grand Rapids, Michigan, USA

First published in the UK in 2007 by Monarch Books
(a publishing imprint of Lion Hudson plc),
Mayfield House, 256 Banbury Road, Oxford OX2 7DH
Tel: +44 (0) 1865 302750   Fax: +44 (0) 1865 302757
Email: monarch@lionhudson.com
www.lionhudson.com

Distributed by:
UK: Marston Book Services Ltd, PO Box 269,
Abingdon, Oxon OX14 4YN
USA: Kregel Publications, PO Box 2607,
Grand Rapids, Michigan 49501

ISBN: 978-1-85424-770-4 (UK)
ISBN: 978-0-8254-6134-7 (USA)

The text paper used in this book has been made from wood
independently certified as having come from sustainable forests.

British Library Cataloguing Data
A catalogue record for this book is available
from the British Library.

Printed and bound in Great Britain by Cox & Wyman Ltd, Reading.

Contents

Introduction 11

Chapter 1 Responding to God's Grace 21

Chapter 2 God's Sovereign Call 41

Chapter 3 A Presence in Prayer; Power in
           Scripture 59

Chapter 4 Visions, Dreams and Signs 89

Chapter 5 Out of the Jaws of Death 105

Chapter 6 God in the Valley of the Shadow 125

Chapter 7 Healing Signs 147

Chapter 8 Jesus Brings Freedom 175

Chapter 9 The Holy Spirit Transforms 201

Epilogue 231

ReSource works for the renewal of people and churches
for mission in the power of the Holy Spirit – across all
traditions, Churches and denominations, and with an
Anglican distinctive. It publishes resources and a regular
magazine, and offers a team ministry which works at all
levels of the Church, and especially with the local and the
ordinary. Its strategy includes the prophetic, the pastoral
and the missionary. It is based at:

4 Old Station Yard, Abingdon, Oxon OX14 3LD
Phone: 01235 553722
Email: office@resource-arm.net
Website: www.resource-arm.net.

For Rachel

Acknowledgements

My grateful thanks to all those who have shared their stories, and apologies to those whose testimonies I have not been able to use. A few of the contributors, for excellent reasons, requested anonymity. Original contributions for this book are marked with *; the other contributions I have used in previous books.

John Woolmer

Introduction

ARE YOU SERIOUS? Do you have any real evidence for your belief – isn't it just a matter of blind faith? What personal experience have you had of God? Surely it is all in the mind – wishful thinking?

People often ask me these types of question. They are not usually looking for intellectual answers (although I am more than happy to give a reasoned defence for my faith – but that is outside the remit of this book); they are searching for evidence of authentic encounters. That is the basis for this book. I have asked a number of people the simple question: 'If you had five minutes to tell someone about your most vivid encounter(s) with God; what would you say?'

That was the challenge I gave to my contributors. It was based on the words of Peter: 'Always be prepared to give an answer to everyone who asks you to give the reason for the hope that you have' (1 Peter 3:15). Many personal friends, and through them other contacts, have answered; too many to use all of them in this short book. Their stories are wonderfully varied. A few I have used before in other books; most are new to print. I have also included a few older stories which seemed worth retelling.

Some of the encounters are very moving, especially those where faith has been sustained and even strengthened in times of deep of grief; some are remarkable and seem to defy any rational explanation.

Consider the man who, without telling his audience, asked for a collection of exactly £10,000 as a sign that he

11

should go ahead with a new project, or the woman who had a dream of the precise name of a house and an accurate picture of a stained glass window within it which was to be the new centre for their Christian project. She was told how to find the right estate agent, in a town miles away from where they were based. Listen to the leading Muslim who hears the voice of God in his mosque and leaves to get baptized in a nearby church – thereby sacrificing everything that had been dear to him to serve Jesus.

Some of the encounters are less dramatic, but in each of them there is a sense of God's intervention, God's call and God's timing. Each encounter made a profound difference to the person fortunate enough to receive it. Professor Dawkins is singularly unimpressed by this sort of argument. He writes:

> The argument from personal experience is the one that is most convincing to those who claim to have had one. But it is the least convincing to anyone else, especially anyone knowledgeable about psychology. Many people believe in God because they have seen a vision of him – or of an angel or a virgin in blue – with their own eyes. Or he speaks to them inside their heads.
>
> You say you have experienced God directly? Well, some people have experienced a pink elephant, but that probably doesn't impress you.[1]

He goes on to cite the case of Peter Sutcliffe, the Yorkshire Ripper, hearing the voice of Jesus telling him to kill women. He cites people who are humoured and locked up because they think they are Charlie Chaplin or Napoleon. He continues (here he is quoting from *The End of Faith*).[2]

Religious experiences are different only in that the people who claim them are numerous... And yet, it is merely an accident of history that is considered normal in society to believe that the Creator of the universe can hear your thoughts, while it is demonstrative of mental illness to believe that he is communicating with you by having the rain tap in Morse code on your bedroom window. And so, while religious people are not generally mad, their core beliefs absolutely are.

Dawkins appears to ignore a number of inconvenient (for him) facts. Men and women who claim to have heard the voice of God, if they are genuine, will allow what they have heard to be tested by others – that rules out Peter Sutcliffe. Those who suffer from serious mental illness need constant care and, sadly, can seldom lead useful lives. They are ill and the fact that they often use religious language doesn't tell us anything about the truth or falsehood of religion.

By contrast, Christians who claim to have heard the voice of God invariably devote themselves unselfishly to the service of others. People with serious mental illnesses often have long periods of clinical illness. Christians who claim to hear the voice of God only hear it occasionally – most of the time their guidance is from prayer, meditation, Scripture, worship, other people and generally less dramatic means.

Also, it is not an accident of history that people believe in a God who communicates with them – it is part of the experience and beliefs of most forms of society. This suggests that it is something endemic to the human race; a quality which distinguishes the human race from apes and their other near relatives. The most probable explanation is that, far from being a delusion, this was something implanted by God. With the hypothesis that God exists and communicates with his people, these experiences make sense. With the hypothesis that God doesn't exist, these experiences are very strange. Dawkins explains these phenomena by what he calls 'a virus of the mind'; the difficulty for his argument is that these experiences are independent of each other and, in many cases, completely unexpected by those who received them.

Guidance Brings a Change of Career

Guidance is given to us in a number of ways. The most common are through the words of Scripture, in prayer (alone or with others), in worship, through words of prophetic insight, through nature and through other members of the body of Christ. Guidance needs to be tested: God invariably confirms his word. When he speaks, he leaves us in little doubt that he has spoken.

Sometimes guidance is very clear; sometimes we have to use our spiritual common sense and take a decision trusting that God will overrule it if we have made a wrong choice. I have received very clear guidance about the question of ordination (see below), and about one particular job (see chapter 4). I have often received guidance in healing and deliverance situations (see chapters 7 and 8); sometimes I have received guidance and spiritual insight through nature (see chapter 3); on many other occasions I have sought guidance and nothing clear has been forthcoming.

In Scripture, one of the clearest and most specific examples was that given to the reluctant Ananias (Acts 9:11–12): 'Go to the house of Judas on Straight Street and ask for a man from Tarsus named Saul, for he is praying. In a vision he has seen a man named Ananias come and place his hands on him to restore his sight'. Knowing Saul of Tarsus by reputation, Ananias could not believe that he was hearing the voice of God. However, after a second word from the Lord, he obeyed, and the rest is history.

One of the books which influenced me in my first few years as a Christian was David Wilkerson's *The Cross and the Switchblade*. In the opening chapter Wilkerson agreed with God that he would exchange two hours a day of television for two hours of prayer – if his advert to sell the TV was answered within an hour of the paper with the advert appearing on the street. His wife commented laconically, 'It sounds as if you don't want to do all that praying'. The TV was sold in the fifty-ninth minute and David Wilkerson's prayer time led to the now world-famous adventure amongst the teenagers hooked on drugs in New York.

That book was laced with extraordinary guidance and other miraculous signs. I used to read it in the junior chapel when I was a teacher at Winchester College, and a number of boys commented that it was the only thing that they remembered from their chapel-going! It certainly affected me. For the first time in my life, I began to consider the possibility that God might choose to speak directly to me. He certainly needed to if I was to leave my comfortable and very fulfilling teaching career!

Saturday Night and Sunday Morning

Marriage and ordination are two of the most important issues that can face the young Christian. On the evening of Saturday 5 August 1967, I faced both. I was on a two week holiday in the Lake District with an Oxford parish.

For the last four years, I had been teaching maths at Winchester College. It had been an enjoyable and challenging time. I was involved, with other senior members of the department, in writing an important new course, called SMP – Schools' Mathematics Project; I had also become a lay reader in the Anglican Church and I was beginning to be involved in the school chapel. I had a great desire to see some much greater signs of faith in a somewhat sceptical school – but could see no real way that this could happen.

For about a year, I had begun to wrestle with the possibility of ordination. As an only child and a shy bachelor, I was well suited to working in the rather protected atmosphere of an English boarding school. I felt very uncomfortable at the thought of being pitched into the real world of parish life.

About two weeks earlier, at the end of the summer term, I had prayed and then made a challenge, on my knees before God, 'If you want me to be ordained you had better make it clear!' My profound hope was that he would answer with a resounding 'No!'

The parish house party had already run for a week. During that time, I had made some input with short talks and, more significantly, had met D. We had formed an instant and quite intense friendship. She was an Oxford undergraduate, very intelligent and challenging. Things had come to a head when we had spent much of the week and most of the Saturday together. We were obviously attracted to one another and shared a similar outlook on the faith.

As we talked, I realized that there was an intense block in the way of any future relationship. Gradually it emerged – she had a serious boyfriend. Worse than that – they had just become engaged. I was devastated. That evening, in the solace of my single bedroom, I sought God's will with a rare intensity. I was angry: 'God – once again my relationships with the opposite sex are heading for disaster!' And I was serious: 'Lord – what is your will?'

As I prayed, and cried, I felt God's presence with an intensity that I wasn't familiar with. God seemed to be saying three things. First, D is not my choice for you; nor you for her. Get out of her life and stop complicating it. Secondly, while you are in the business of giving things up, give up your precious teaching career and do what I want you to do. Thirdly, read Psalm 143. As I did so, I particularly noticed verse 8 which said something to the effect of 'I will show you my loving kindness in the morning'.

I continued, far into the night, in fervent prayer. God seemed to assure me that he would not allow me to be hurt unbearably. I was also very concerned for the complications that I was now causing to D. I fell asleep, strangely confident that things would become clear in the morning.

On the Sunday morning, which was also the Feast of the Transfiguration in the Anglican calendar, the house party went to Ambleside parish church. The first thing I remember is that we sang Psalm 143. As a mathematician, I rated that as 149:1 against! I was very conscious of God's presence and was, I think, expecting guidance from the sermon.

The preacher, the rector of the Oxford parish, was an effective evangelist. Normally, he would have used the opportunity of a church full of holiday makers to make a powerful evangelistic call. He knew me well, but he was completely unaware of my thinking about ordination. He didn't preach evangelistically, but chose to speak about the Transfiguration of Jesus.

He mentioned that, as Jesus came down from the mountain, humanly he had a choice. He could return to Galilee as a fairly successful minor prophet, or he could go up to Jerusalem – obeying God's call – which was a far harder choice. Then the speaker turned to us. He continued 'In a much smaller way, some of you face the same sort of choice. You can stay where you are and be fairly successful or you can obey God's call to do something which you think is far harder!'

I sensed the presence of God in a way that I had experienced at the time of my conversion and which I have also experienced, from time to time, in later years. I knew he was speaking to me. I knew that this was his answer to my year of searching.

I could have talked my way out of the previous night as sheer emotionalism; I could have argued that the morning was just coincidence and that the sermon applied to others and not to me. But the two together, like two sides of a coin, were indivisible. I had prayed and God had graciously answered.

I left the church and went for a long walk. Spiritually, I was high up on the mountain top. Practically and emotionally, I was confused. I still hoped that there might be a way out. I was reluctant to abandon my new friendship with D. I hoped that perhaps the church would turn me down. But I knew that I had no choice; I must offer myself for ordination and see what happened.

The friendship that I had formed with D lasted through the second week of the house party and continued for a short while afterwards. With hindsight, it would have been wiser and easier for us both if I had given it up immediately. When God speaks, he expects obedience!

In the autumn, I began the long process of offering myself for selection as an ordination candidate in the Church of

England. Despite the clarity of the call, I was still reluctant to take the step.

Postscript

In the spring of 1969, I went to help on an Oxford student party at Lee Abbey. There I met Jane. We were married in 1974 and now have four grown-up children who are all convinced Christians. Later in 1969, I started on what was called a schoolmaster's ordination course. My mother had just died and the course was not a success. After a further family tragedy later in that year, I then had a year at St John's College, Nottingham before returning to Winchester first as an ordained mathematician and then as a chaplain. In the autumn of 1974, we saw quite a revival in the school. Mark Stibbe's book *Thinking Clearly about Revival* tells how the revival lasted some seven years and led a number of members of the school to leadership in the Christian church. Soon afterwards, I left school-teaching.

I went on to do a normal curacy in Oxford. God has been very good and I have, despite many failures and failings, seen some wonderful things in Oxford, Shepton Mallet and overseas, especially in Zambia. I am very grateful that he chose to answer my prayer offered, in some haste, in July 1967.

From time to time, I have experienced his presence with the same sort of intensity. Once it came before the mission in the school in 1974, once it came when I was seeking guidance about whether or not to accept the living in Shepton Mallet; on other occasions it has come during times of worship and ministry – particularly in some situations which have involved deliverance of people or buildings from dark powers.

Years later, I met D again. I was conducting the marriage of the daughter of one of my parishioners to her son. She had had a very happy marriage, but was now widowed. We were glad to meet again, albeit very briefly.

I am conscious how much more interesting and fulfilled my life has become and what a privilege it is to serve God and his people in full-time ministry. I am also amazed how God has changed my personality. The shy bachelor schoolmaster, immersed in mathematics, is largely gone and I now enjoy meeting people from many different backgrounds. I have had some of my most wonderful experiences overseas in rural Africa, Argentina and Papua New Guinea.

I am very doubtful that, without the Ambleside encounter, I would have ever have had either the will or the courage to offer myself for ordination.

Notes

1 Richard Dawkins, *The God Delusion*, Bantam Press, 2006, p. 88
2 Richard Dawkins, *A Devil's Chaplain*, Weidenfeld and Nicolson, 2003.

1

Responding to God's Grace

[Eric Delve*/Jane Holloway*/Richard Harvey*/Sue Hesselwood*/Muslim woman in Asia*]

IF YOU OBSERVE THE CHRYSALIS of a butterfly, you will eventually see the future colours of the upper wings; then the chrysalis will darken, cracks will appear on the case and the insect will emerge. Some conversions are like that – you can sense that the Holy Spirit is with a person (John 14:17b) long before they are aware of what is happening.

Sometimes a chrysalis colours up, but for some inexplicable reason the butterfly never emerges from it. Evangelism can be like that: someone seems interested, and even responsive, but they never seem ready to make a real commitment to Jesus. In time, their interest often goes cold; the evangelist retreats disappointed, hoping that someone else will take up the challenge where he or she has apparently failed.

Occasionally, people are converted from nowhere. They have a dream, or some other sudden unexpected, and usually unsought, encounter. Like Saul of Tarsus (see Acts 9), they appear to have no choice. God has called them and they must respond.

I have divided the testimonies about conversion into two chapters – this chapter deals with the more normal 'caterpillar to butterfly' type of conversion; the next gives some rather more obviously supernatural encounters.

Caterpillars represent us in our natural state – they are concerned with eating and survival. If necessary, they will destroy other smaller caterpillars in order to protect their food plant. The Bible clearly teaches that without Christ we are naturally selfish. The chrysalis represents a transitional stage; there is an apparent death to the past and the expectation of something new. The butterfly has essentially the same body as the caterpillar; but is free to feed, rest and reproduce. In Christ we have a similar freedom and, hopefully, a desire to evangelize.

The Bible makes it clear that God's sovereignty is at work in all true conversions; it also teaches that we all need to respond with an act of repentance and faith. The test of all this is not dramatic signs but a fruitful life. Jesus makes this clear at the end of the Sermon on the Mount (see Matthew 7:15–23 and John 15:1–17).

The first of my stories tells how a young man's rebellion against a very strict Christian upbringing was graciously dealt with by an encounter with the living God.

*   *   *

Eric Delve *is Vicar of St Luke's, Maidstone, England – a thriving Anglican church. For many years he has also travelled as an evangelist, speaking and leading missions. Married to Pat for forty-three years, he has six children and four grandchildren. He also conducts leadership seminars and conferences for men. His story is of a strict Christian upbringing, a lengthy period of rebellion and then an encounter with the God of grace.*

Being born in 1942 and growing up in the aftermath of the Second World War means that my life demonstrates that in the past we lived in a very different country. Not only was the society of 1940s and 1950s Britain very different from today, I was also raised in a peculiar social cultural backwater.

My parents were sincere believers in Jesus Christ and members of the group of people referred to as 'The Brethren'. Although originally descended from a group known as the Plymouth Brethren, they had separated from this highly exclusive group, and preferred to be known as the Christian Brethren. This may seem archaic and irrelevant, but it was very much the culture in which I grew up. The little world of the Christian Brethren formed my universe.

My mother's background was a rather troubled one and she had found enormous comfort in her conversion to Jesus Christ. It had brought about a revolution in her life but, at the time of her marriage to my father, she was still negotiating the need for healing from horrendous abuse in her early life.

When she became pregnant she was delighted, but what she really wanted was a little girl. Consequently, I was somewhat of a disappointment. When I was three my mother finally received what she had wanted – the little girl whom she could dress up and whose hair she could curl, without meeting any kind of masculine resistance. I think it is more than possible that my mother's delight in the arrival of my sister sowed in me the seeds of a profound sense of rejection, which was not truly justified, but then little children very rarely understand the motivations or grasp the good intentions of their parents.

High standards of behaviour were of course very much the expectation not only of the surrounding culture, but especially of the micro-culture of the Brethren. I did sincerely try to be a good boy, but the conflicting sense of rejection deep within and the anger that I felt kept emerging and I found myself to be distressingly naughty. I wanted to be breathtakingly changed, and I frequently repented, because I'd been told that if I gave my heart to Jesus, sweetness, love, light, joy, peace, etc would flood through me. I did so and was profoundly disappointed to discover that I was not flooded with the aforementioned qualities. I concluded that I hadn't done it right, so did it again. In fact I did it on numerous occasions. I was aware that Jesus died on a cross so that I could be offered forgiveness by grace, but I was also aware that, as a Christian, I was supposed to be living a godly and holy life, which I manifestly was not.

The conflict within me continued to grow as I grew. My grandmother famously observed to one of my aunts, 'They are going to have trouble with that boy', and I suppose it's true that they did have trouble with 'that boy'. Corporal punishment was of course the norm in virtually every house in our area, and our house was no different. My mother, however, despaired of being able to inculcate into me any discipline. Having bought a special cane for delivering the corporal punishment, she then broke it over me; for some reason I felt unaccountably guilty that I had caused such distress, as she burst into tears, saying, 'What on earth am I going to do with you?'

It was of course unfair on my father that I became, like so many other children, subject to the common threat 'You wait 'til your father comes home'. It was unfair because my father often had to administer discipline to me for something that had happened hours before, and of which he had no first hand knowledge, and of course it meant that my experience of him was unduly coloured by the fact that he was administering punishment more frequently than his personal experience of me warranted. In my teens I would argue furiously with him and, almost alone amongst our family, I could reduce him to near apoplexy.

In spite of these conflicts I became a youth leader and worked in the youth fellowship at church. After marriage at the age of twenty-one, I continued to serve God in this way. However, I still desperately longed for the affirmation that somehow would confirm to me that I really was lovable, not horrible. By this time I knew that my mother truly loved me; indeed that she adored me, but the sense of rejection from early childhood never seemed to go away. Consequently my behaviour continued to be a grave disappointment to me, particularly because of my constant chasing after members of the opposite sex – the powerful hormonal drive of late teens and early twenties, combined with an insecure longing for the affirmation of women. All this meant that I was beyond my own control. Even after marriage, this behaviour continued and, of course, I was wracked by guilt.

Eventually this all reached a crisis point where I cracked and began to tell God just what I really thought of him. Frankly, I just couldn't stand it any more. Whatever heaven was like, I was pretty sure it was going to be the religious nonsense that was driving me completely bananas, and I didn't want it, and I told God so. It was like the bursting of a dam. I raged at God for at least thirty-six hours, with a short break for sleep. I swore and cursed, telling him I didn't care if he sent me to hell, as long as I could just get this stuff off my chest, and tell him how much I'd hated being brought up as a Christian; how it felt to me like I was a wild eagle in a cage, longing to break free, and chained to the ground by this so-called message of grace.

Finally I arrived at a point where I was almost exhausted and stopped. Extraordinarily, from deep within, I heard a quiet voice say, 'Is that all?' I said, 'No, there's a bit more and you can have that,' and continued my tirade until I was truly, finally, absolutely exhausted. Certain that I had completely blown it and was now destined for hell, I sensed this gentle voice saying, 'Is that it then?' I replied, 'Yes, that's it,' and the voice came again – 'Shall we get on with it then?'

For the first time in my life I realized that God really was a God of grace. I knew at last that none of my sins was a surprise to him and, once confessed, they were not a barrier. I also understood for the very first time in my life that God really did love me. This wasn't just some few spare drops of his love, over and above his love for the entire world, but deeply personal, passionate and total. I have had other moments of despair and anger since that time, but never again seriously doubted the truth of his love.

However, it took a long while for me to process what had happened. I began to recognize that the voice I'd heard was not so much the voice of Jesus, the man who had died for me. As I read the New Testament, he was becoming more and more of a hero to me and I think it is true to say that I fell in love with him. However, I realized that the voice that had asked me with such extraordinary calm and peace 'Shall we get on with it then?' was the voice of the Father – the heavenly Father whose love for me was rooted in a passionate desire to believe in me and not a longing to punish me.

Even writing these words brings tears to my eyes. Like so many wartime babies my early experience of life had left me effectively without a dad and this day had opened the door for me to know at last there was a real father who was mine. It began a journey for me that was to lead to a total healing of my relationship with my earthly dad, to the point that when he died in 2006 it was the most profound loss of my life. Everything flowed from the day that I discovered God's grace is bigger and more effective than all my anger, rebellion and hate.

I hear that when Karl Barth, the great theologian, was asked by a student at the end of a lecture 'Professor Barth, what is the greatest discovery you ever made in the field of theology?' he replied, 'Jesus loves me – this I know, for the Bible tells me so.' I understand. It's the greatest discovery I've made and it has never ceased to amaze me.

* * *

Jane Holloway *currently works as National Prayer Director at the World Prayer Centre, Birmingham, which seeks to mobilize prayer across the nation and the world.*

How can I really put my trust in a God if I am not sure he is really there? That was one of the many questions I was raising on the evening in March 1977 in my friend Mary's home in Dunedin, New Zealand. I did not have to wait long as that question was answered by the Father himself in the early hours of the next morning. My encounter with him on 25 March 1977 changed my life for ever!

Up to that point, I would probably have considered myself a Christian. I had been brought up in a home where going to the local Anglican church on the farm (in England) was part of my father's family's lifestyle. I had also attended, as a part of my secondary education, a lovely Catholic boarding school which was run on Christian values. I had taken my religious education O level and passed with a grade A. I had always believed that there was 'a God' and that was as far as it went.

After taking my A levels, I had come to the conclusion that I did not want to do any more studying. So I spent a year learning administrative and secretarial skills and then embarked on a career as a PA. I started my first job in 1972, working as PA to a retired Professor of Biochemistry at Oxford University – Sir Hans Krebs, a German Jewish Nobel Laureate. I was part of his team of research scientists and technicians that had been working together since Sir Hans had to flee Hitler in the late 1930s.

Mary had arrived on a scholarship from New Zealand to join the team and do a DPhil degree, and over the next three years we became good friends as we enjoyed many similar interests. Mary was a committed Christian and I knew she went to church regularly, but she never forced her faith on me. A typical Kiwi, she was very proud of her nation and invited me to come out to stay with her when she returned to be a lecturer in biochemistry at Dunedin University. So I saved my money and left working for 'the Prof' and went to spend five months staying with Mary, touring around New Zealand and looking up long-lost relations.

New Zealand is the most spectacularly beautiful country I had ever seen. Geography had been my favourite subject at school and I simply could not believe that I was able to visit most of the nation, experiencing the wonder and beauty of how it was formed with such a diversity of plant, animal and bird life. Whether it was sitting next to an albatross and watch it preparing to fly, seeing the yellow-eyed penguins try to climb a cliff, experiencing a sunset over the Southern Alps, walking on a ninety-mile-long beach, climbing up a glacier and 'hearing it moving'; smelling the hot springs, geysers and volcanoes in action – I was simply blown away by it all. Towards the end of my time in NZ, we visited a small church, built in the middle of the forest in the Southern Alps near the Franz Joseph Glacier, made out of tree ferns – with its east window facing the glacier. As we walked in, I felt an incredible peace and went to look in the visitors' book. Every entry I could read in English said, in effect, 'God is here. God is in this place.' I remember being forced to stop and sit in the pews quietly for a moment, awed by what I was sensing, but then got up and moved on quickly not sure what that was all about!

It all came to a head on Sunday 24 March. It was nearing the end of my five-month visit. Mary had made the decision to take me not to her Baptist church, but to an Anglican church in Dunedin on that Sunday evening. We had arrived and for the first time in my life I felt that I did not fit into what was happening. Yes, I knew the liturgy and the hymns but something was different. Mary had realized that I had sensed that and we therefore had had a long conversation into the night about some of my fears about returning back to the UK and about God – was he really there? From what I remember we ended in the early hours of the Monday and just as I was about to go to bed, I sensed an incredible presence enter the room. I could not see anything, but I was completely overawed. It was the sort of presence that was powerful, awesome and seemed to fill the whole space. I recall that 'we' then had a 'conversation'.

'Will you follow me, Jane?' These were the words that echoed in my mind. I don't remember what I thought, but I do remember an incredible battle that was going on inside me. I seemed to wrestle with this for ages – I have no idea how long for. Then again another sentence: 'This will be the hardest decision you will make'. Again I wrestled. What was going on? I found myself blurting out 'I'll try'. Immediately I was overtaken with a profound sense of peace; all my anxieties were gone. I felt draped in this peace and as Mary had already gone off to bed, I staggered to my room and fell asleep.

The next morning when I woke and drew back the curtains, the whole of Dunedin looked different. It was all in colour – bright, bold colours. I felt I had been given a new pair of eyes and the ones before had been set to black and white. For the next few days, it was hard for Mary and me to talk as another friend of mine had arrived to stay. But she reassured me that she knew God was on my case. I didn't quite know what that would mean, but felt led to go to a second-hand bookshop in Dunedin and buy a book on the Christian faith which helped me over the next few weeks as I travelled back to the UK.

When I returned to the UK and to my family, I went out and bought a Bible. I chose the Good News version as it had pictures, and a reading guide at the back. Over the following weeks and months God himself taught me how to read it, how to talk to him throughout each day and how I was to ask him for guidance. Mary wrote to me faithfully each week encouraging me on my new-found faith. I found a job in Oxford, a house to share, and then after six months felt the prompting by God to link up with other Christians. A wonderful 'beginners group' at a large church in Oxford – St Aldates – provided both the encouragement to grow in my new-found Christian faith, and that church became my home for the next nine years. And after a year – after another encounter with God in a time of prayer – I felt called to join the staff to work as PA to the rector, Michael Green.

And the rest – as they say – is history: over eight years on the staff of St Aldates; five years working as outreach coordinator (evangelism and drama) at Regent College, Vancouver,

Canada; two years with Springboard across the UK (evangelism and mission) and then for the last thirteen years working in the whole area of prayer mobilization and evangelism (with Crosswinds, Evangelical Alliance and now with the World Prayer Centre in Birmingham). I have had the privilege of travelling in many parts of the world, seeing the Holy Spirit 'in action' like the stories we read in the Acts of the Apostles and working with some fantastic people. I have been a member of some wonderful churches in the different places I have lived. All this happened because of an encounter in the early morning of 25 March 1977 when our heavenly Father came in search of one of his children. I am so grateful to him for showing me himself. I am so grateful in the way that he communicated with me, as that has helped me so much as I have sought to share him with others and to encourage the mobilization of prayer.

'Ask and it will be given to you; seek and you will find; knock and the door will be opened to you' (Mat 7:7). That was the verse that Mary shared with me on 24 March 1977 and I have come to understand, believe and know that our Father is true to his word and that he longs to meet us, help us and resource us – when we open our hearts fully to his love.

* * *

Richard Harvey *is a Jewish believer in Jesus who became a Christian at Winchester College through the evangelistic ministry of Canon Keith de Berry (then Rector of St Aldates, Oxford). He has worked with the Church's Ministry among the Jewish People (CMJ) and Jews for Jesus, and is a founding member of the London Messianic Congregation. He now teaches the Hebrew Bible and Jewish Studies at All Nations*

Christian College, a missionary training college, and is married to Monica, who is also a Jewish believer in Jesus.

In the final months of my grandfather's life I used to visit him regularly, as the Central London church where I was based as an evangelist was just around the corner from where he lived. He was a man of the world, a successful stockbroker and businessman, with strong connections to the Jewish world but no personal faith. Now at the age of seventy-eight his health had seriously declined, and he did not have long to live.

I had always been in awe of him. He came originally from Germany, where, in Essen, the Hirschland family were a leading family: founders of the local synagogue, benefactors of the community, and with banking and commercial interests. His father had come to England before the Second World War, and my grandfather had continued the family business and integrated into British society, changing the family name from Hirschland to Harvey to avoid German and Jewish overtones at a time when Britain was at war. As a businessman, and also in his family life, he had been hard-headed, ruthless and successful, but had left a trail of difficult relationships behind him.

When I became a Christian, he, like others in my family, was not impressed. But he had always taken an interest in my education and choice of becoming a missionary; even once offering to 'help me' by asking a Bishop he had befriended on one of his frequent cruises to 'further my progress'.

I had been praying for the opportunity to share the gospel with him, but had not had the nerve to broach the subject. As with other members of my family, I knew that my becoming a Christian had not been well received, but had tried to be a dutiful grandson and was longing to share my faith with him. At the end of one of our visits, as I got up from his bedside and was about to leave the room, I said to him, 'I'm praying for you, Grandfather.' Imagine my surprise when he replied 'Oh yes, I think we had better – what do I say?' Instead of hearing 'I'm praying for you', he had heard me say 'Shall we pray together?' or some such invitation. In a way that was wholly unexpected and unplanned, he wanted to pray with me.

Although this was the moment I had been longing for, I did not know what to do. He did not have a strong religious background in Judaism, so I asked him if he knew the Lord's Prayer. He did, and we said it together. I did not know what to do next, but he then said to me, 'Why is it important about Jesus?' I replied by explaining that it was only when we put our trust in Jesus that we could be sure we would go to be with God when we die, and that by accepting him as our Lord and saviour we could know we were forgiven for all the things that we had done wrong. 'Oh yes, I see,' he replied, and just as he would have clinched one of his business deals in his earlier life, he added, 'Would you like a glass of sherry?'

I knew that for him, the penny had dropped. He had opened his life up to God and had accepted Jesus as his Lord, saviour and Messiah. Although this came right at the end of his life (for he died just a month or so after this), he had acknowledged God and accepted Jesus in a way that he would never have been prepared to do in his earlier years. I felt a great sense of relief that he too, like me, had come to know the Messiah of Israel. He is one of the many members of my family who have come to know Jesus, although as with most Jewish families, there are many who do not yet acknowledge him. But you are never too old to come to know the Messiah of Israel and saviour of the world!

*   *   *

Sue Hesselwood *was a teacher, married Trevor in her early forties and is used much in leading prayer ministries which have helped many people. She and Trevor are trustees of The Well at Leamington Spa – a place which has been much used in the healing ministry locally and further afield.*

I was brought up in a church-going family, which for me meant that I cannot remember ever not believing in God. As a young child I suffered from recurring attacks of bronchitis, which meant that I was often in bed for days at a time. Sometimes, when I felt really sick, I would talk to Jesus, and I knew that he was with me.

In my late teens (1966) I went to Portsmouth for three years to train as a teacher. I got involved in the Christian Union at the college and one Friday I found myself at an evangelistic coffee evening. During the general discussion after the speaker had finished, I tried to persuade a non-believer that Jesus was alive. I said something like 'Jesus died and rose again. He didn't die again the next day, or the next week, or the next year, or a hundred years later – he stayed alive through the centuries and is alive today!' In the middle of saying this I felt an overwhelming sense of the presence of God. It was as if He was saying, 'That's right. I am alive. You have always known me in your head. Now you are experiencing my presence.' Later, in my room, I knelt down in awe. Eventually I said something like 'God, that was really you. Please don't ever let me go.'

It was several years before I experienced the presence of God again, but that evening in Portsmouth was the start of a journey of faith, based not on my choosing to believe, but on the absolute certainty that God existed and that He had revealed Himself to me.

In 1977/8 I went out with Trevor for about six months. I felt attracted to him, but deep down, I never felt it was really 'me' who was going out with him, and there was a sense in which I was glad when each date was over, as then I didn't have to play-act any more.

Eventually, I broke off the relationship. This reaction in me towards Trevor was just a stronger version of what was going on with all my relationships, deep or superficial – I kept everyone at arm's length and acted a part. I knew I was doing it, but just didn't know what to do about it, so I ignored it and kept myself busy with my teaching and involvement in my church.

A few years later I suffered a nervous breakdown. Prayer, medication and relaxation therapy brought healing, and I was able to return to work. About this time I went to a Christian conference at the NEC near Birmingham. At the end of one meeting, the speaker asked all those who felt that they weren't going anywhere because their lives kept going round in circles, to move to the front of the hall so that she could pray. 'That's me,' I thought, and walked to the front. As soon as the speaker started praying I began to shake from head to toe, like a pneumatic drill. I wasn't frightened. I knew it was God doing something, and I wanted to cooperate with him as much as I could. Eventually the prayer stopped, and I stopped shaking.

At the end of the conference I went home and continued life as normal – except that, gradually, I began to realize that something was different – somehow I didn't need to keep people at arm's length any more as the 'real me' was now able to make relationships with people in a natural way. I could only put it down to the fact that in my 'pneumatic drill' experience, God had released whatever had been stopping me from being really 'me'. The consequence of this dawned on me one night in bed – I could now contemplate a long-term relationship with Trevor (if he still wanted one)! To cut a long story short, Trevor and I resumed going out together in November 1988, and were married in August 1989. We have been happily married ever since.

An Illness for God's Glory

I have always been surprised by Jesus' statement in John 9:3 that the man was born blind 'so that the work of God might be displayed in his life'. Here is a recent example where this text was quoted by someone from a different faith! The story comes from a Wycliffe Bible translator working in a sensitive area (hence the lack of details and changed name).

'It is a sin for me to pray in Jesus' Name. I am a Muslim,' Brenda [not her real name] told me. A woman from Central Asia, she had sold many of her possessions in a desperate attempt to find medical help for her six-year-old daughter, whom I will call Lily. The search in her country was in vain, and the doors in Russia were slammed shut. She lost all hope of seeing her daughter run and play, like a healthy child.

As a missionary and friend of the family, I had been praying: asking what God would have me to do in this situation. He sent me an answer in the form of a Christmas card and very generous cheque 'for my ministry' from someone I had only met once in my life. I knew this cheque was intended by him for a special little girl. The search began for the needed medical attention, and a year later we landed in Oxford, England, where God brought together everything needed to treat this young girl's various health problems.

Brenda did not mind if I prayed to Jesus, so I prayed before each meal we shared. She even came to church with me in Oxford. Of course, the service needed to be translated from English into the language of her heart. Brenda decided she wanted to read the Bible for herself.

'I found the answer to my question!' she announced to me one day. She had been reading John 9, where the disciples brought a blind man to Jesus and said, 'Who sinned, this man or his parents, that he was born blind?' Jesus replied, 'It was not because of his sins or his parents' sins. He was born blind so that the power of God could be seen in him.' Since the day that Lily's medical problems were discovered, Brenda had wondered in her heart, 'Why my daughter? What did I do to deserve this?' God spoke to her and assured that her daughter's problems were not a punishment, but an instrument of his grace and a channel for his glory to be revealed.

Over the previous year, Brenda had encountered the provision and care of God as over £18,000 came pouring in from strangers to cover Lily's medical expenses. She saw the power of God even before she and her daughter arrived in England, as one by one God opened the doors for their visas, safe travel, housing, and provided a world-renowned specialist doctor willing to perform the needed operation.

'Mummy, it's your turn to pray tonight,' her daughter said unexpectedly as we sat down to dinner. It was the same day Brenda had found her answer. A sheepish look came over Brenda's face, but I assured her that God does not accept prayers according to their eloquence, but according to their sincerity. Then Brenda prayed in Jesus' name!

Since that day she has confessed her sins and has believed that Jesus' death on the cross was in her place, and that his resurrection brings her life. She now knows the only true God and his son Jesus Christ, whom he sent. As she continues to read his Word, she often tells me, 'I think God put this verse in here just for me!' The Holy Spirit opened Brenda's eyes so that as she witnessed inexplicable generosity and a quiet testimony of faith lived out before her, she encountered the Living God.

Conclusion

The Bible is clear that each conversion takes place through an act of divine grace. 'You did not choose me, but I chose you,' said Jesus. The last story illustrates that point very clearly! The evidence for a true conversion is what Jesus called fruit (see John 15:16, Matthew 7:16). Fruit, in Scripture, means a number of things. A changed character which exhibits the fruit of the Spirit (Galatians 5:22–23) is the most obvious and the most attractive. But fruit also refers to evangelism (see Romans 1:13 where the English word 'harvest' is used for the same Greek word translated 'fruit' elsewhere); to good works (Colossians 1:10) and to worship (Hebrews 13:15).

The genuineness of any profession of faith should be tested against the fruit that is born in the new life of discipleship. Nevertheless, a good clear testimony is a great help in building a life of discipleship. Jesus taught the disciples that the Holy Spirit 'lives with you and will be in you'

(John 14:17). Many people who have had more gradual conversion experiences are well aware of that truth. They know something of God but have not yet received him in their hearts by faith (Ephesians 3:17).

Some butterflies spend a very long time as a chrysalis, for others that period of the life cycle is quite short. As we have seen in these accounts, God deals with each individual quite differently. In a true spiritual experience, God doesn't build religious clones, as the cults do, but creates individuals uniquely stamped and sealed (Ephesians 1:13) by the gift of his indwelling Spirit.

2

God's Sovereign Call

[Fred Lemon/Muslim leader/Peter*/Mike Hutchinson*/
Don Latham*]

ALL CONVERSIONS ARE A SUPERNATURAL act of God's grace. Some are so dramatic that the fortunate recipient seems to have little, if any, choice. The first two stories in this chapter, and Ian McCormack's (chapter 5), fall into that category. We can only hear them and marvel at the clarity and power of God's call. The next two accounts are from two people that I know well. Both have had an encounter in which the presence of God, in a tangible form, was very real. The final story illustrates how healing and evangelism are closely linked, and shows the remarkable power of a miracle to affect other people.

*   *   *

I heard **Fred Lemon** *give his testimony in Oxford Town Hall. It was at a healing meeting led by my old friend Fred Smith. Fred Smith was no stranger to miracles – even that night a man walked in yellow with cancer, walked out looking very well, and when I contacted him some months later said that he had been completely healed; but it was Fred Lemon who had the strangest story. It ran something like this – a more detailed account can be found in his book,* Breakout.

In my younger days, I was a serious criminal. One day, with some others, I robbed a jeweller's shop in London. Unfortunately, there was some violence; we left the jeweller almost dead. Soon afterwards, we were arrested and brought to trial. The jeweller's life hung in the balance, so did mine. If he had died, according to the law at the time, we would have certainly been hanged.

Fortunately he recovered; I was given a long stretch, and ended up in Dartmoor. It was a gloomy terrible place, and I made little attempt to socialise or to get educated. I was one of the most hopeless cases, among a group of desperate lost people. Then on 10 August 1950, I awoke to find three men standing in front of me in my cell. It was in the middle of the night, but the dark gloomy cell was flooded with light.

The angel on the right said, 'Fred, this is Jesus,' pointing to the figure in the middle. I was aware of the presence of Jesus. He started to tell me all about my past life. Strangely, I didn't feel afraid. He told me how he had died to pay the penalty for my sins, and through his resurrection that he had overcome the power of death.

Significantly, at the end of a wonderful speech, he said, 'If you want to become a Christian, you must drive the hatred from your heart.' I knew that he was speaking the truth. I was well aware that I had an extreme hatred, especially towards some of the prison warders, and that I had even contemplated attempting to murder some of them. I had been listening with my head in my hands, but with this last sentence I looked up; the three men still looking at me were fading through the wall. There was a distinct click, and I was alone. I knew that Jesus and two of his angels had chosen to visit me. I wasn't afraid. In fact, immediately, I lay down and fell into a deep and peaceful sleep.

Fred went on to tell how his life had been instantly transformed by God's grace. It hadn't been easy, in many ways people found the new Fred more difficult to understand than the old one. Years later, after his release, Fred Lemon wrote a book, called *Breakout*, and liked nothing better than to travel around giving his testimony to God's grace, and telling of the unexpected visitors in his prison cell.

The Voice of God and the Muslim Leader

Conversion to Christianity is very costly for people of other faiths – especially Muslims. But sometimes God speaks so clearly – even more clearly than by the sending of an angel – that there seems to be no choice. The man in question is now training for full-time Christian work. This testimony was written for me by a prominent Anglican, who is involved in the work of mission and renewal, and who has met 'A' and heard him speak. For obvious reasons, we have omitted personal and geographical details. 'A' gave this testimony.

I was trained at the Egyptian Islamic University in sharia law. Then I returned to my home country to study international law at the leading university to study international law. Because I was a radical Muslim, I was being groomed as a future leader and was working amongst international Muslim students. I had the title of Imam in the university mosque.

I became a Christian on Friday 2 September 2001. I had been leading a Muslim prayer meeting. My heart was strong for Islam. We followed the teachings of the Qu'ran and gave converts money; there was also a deliberate process of impregnating Christian girls – who then produced children who would grow up as Muslims. I was very tired – I had coursework to write up for my legal studies. I hid away in a quiet room, recited the Qu'ran and fell asleep while reading my law books. I was woken up by a great wind which was followed with echoes. I heard a voice calling my name three times. The voice said 'I am the Lord – I want you to be saved'. This agreed with what I had heard when having conversations with Christians in Egypt and other places.

I went out to the mosque. I was very angry and I went to take my ritual ablutions. I came back to pray. I emphasized that I was a radical Muslim. As I was still praying, the voice called me again. The walls shook. Glass broke in the windows, and many people ran out of the mosque. Others stayed with me.

The voice continued, 'I am the Lord – Christ Jesus – I want you to be saved.' My heart was very certain that it was God speaking to me because part of my prayer had been that he would make it clear to me what he was saying. I had prayed to Allah and this seemed to be the answer.

I could not become a Christian. I would be killed; I would be unable to finish my legal studies and would betray all my family. They were all staunch Muslims. Shame would fall on my people. I tried to bargain with God. I asked him to give me a year to finish my degree. As I did so, a light came accompanied by great heat. I saw a scroll pictured on the wall. As it unrolled, I read Psalm 56. I rushed out of the mosque. I ran into a Christian church. I found a number of Christians and asked how I could be saved. There were a large group of men and women praying. Men and women together – that was impossible for a Muslim. Worse still, they were wearing shoes. I had no idea where to sit. The whole church stopped praying when they discovered what was happening. They broke out in spontaneous praise to God. They cried out, 'The great Sheik has become a Christian!' I gave my testimony. They said, 'God has called you!' I confessed Jesus Christ as my saviour. I added, 'Christ has brought me to lose everything. I have gone from being a Muslim leader to just being a brother.'

I have lost a lot – that is why I am so serious about it. Soon afterwards I told my girlfriend that I had become a Christian. She told my family, who were astounded. The next day, I was asked to go to the mosque. My family put great pressure on me. I went through the ritual ablutions, but prayed that I would not have to go to the mosque, because I was frightened about returning there. I had a great sense of power and heat. It felt as though I had a fever, people were concerned for my health and I didn't have to go to the mosque. The next day, I told them in the mosque and in my home that I had become a Christian.

My father slapped me and told me to leave home immediately. He said he ought to kill me but that he loved me too much to do that. A Roman Catholic student friend took me into his room because I was now homeless. Later at an international event, journalists wanted to interview me. A little while later, some Muslims shot and killed a friend of mine – mistaking him for me. I am covered with both Christ's and my friend's blood. The murderers were caught and imprisoned; but I have become a foreigner in my own country. Christian brothers and sisters have given me money and lodgings. Others tried to assassinate me. Some came from Libya and Egypt. Twice I was shot, in my stomach and in my leg. But despite being in a coma for two weeks, I have survived. I am now studying at a Bible college in England – financed by a Christian missionary organization.

* * *

Peter *is a university lecturer who specializes in fungi and geology. He has wrestled with depression, but despite this, or perhaps because of it, is able to help and encourage others on their spiritual journey. His powerful experience of a divine presence have transformed his thinking and his life in the twenty-three years since. He is currently involved in a church plant as an assistant cell group leader, member of the healing prayer team, helper with the elderly, part of the service administration team and member of the church council.*

Over twenty years ago I was severely depressed but didn't realize it. My father had died unexpectedly about fifteen months earlier, and as a relatively late entrant to lecturing in the post-Robbins era of university expansion I was a workaholic through anxiety. I was trying to produce research publications while dealing with a busy teaching programme with relatively large classes. We had two young children but were both too busy to have much social life. I was very isolated and communications in the family were poor, although I didn't fully realize it at the time.

I started talking to someone outside the family who seemed to connect with me rapidly and intensely. It was like a switch being thrown in my mind and depression was replaced by feverish activity day and night. I now know it was the start of a hypermanic breakdown.

In the ensuing chaos that I generated in family, friends and neighbourhood, I became aware of a strong presence about me. That day, while alone in the house I asked, 'Who are you?' and a very distant voice said, once only, 'Jesus'. A short while later I was forced on my knees to try to pray and

to submit. The powerful presence stayed, it was both com-
forting and frightening, Suddenly God, Jesus and what I later
realized was the Holy Spirit were very real. I felt compelled
to ring a Christian colleague who worked in the next room
who simply said, 'You are not mad. I will be here when you
need me.'

In twenty-four hours I was changed from being at best an
agnostic, to a very new and raw Christian. Despite the strong
medication, the calming and protective sense of a presence
stayed with me all through the subsequent weeks of recovery
which took place in a large psychiatric hospital some eighty
miles away. The hospital staff team was supportive and never
tried to make me question the reality of my experience. The
chaplains came to see me and I went to their services. There
were no Christian patients I could talk to in my ward; but I
did find one book, *Lord Change Me* by Evelyn Christenson,
which helped me to understand what was happening and
gave me a key verse for life, Romans 8:28: 'And we know that
in all things God works for the good of those who love him'.

The Christian colleague to whom I had spoken greeted me
on my return from hospital with the words 'It is a terrible
thing to fall into the hands of the living God' (Heb: 10:31). He
was my Christian mentor for all the crucial early years. I
started going to the very middle-of-the-road Anglican church
where my children had gone to Sunday school. I learnt to be
an ordinary Christian in the next five years – despite my
crash course in faith, it was not the place where one dis-
cussed, or even mentioned rapid conversion experiences. I
did quite quickly join an adult confirmation class and the
curate introduced me to a lunchtime Christian group of
university colleagues from different churches.

Obviously one might suspect that the whole experience

was just part of the breakdown but all the long-term results indicate otherwise, as they have all been positive. One hard lesson was that finding the reality of God under those conditions meant that I could not trust my thoughts and emotions. I had to rely firstly on what actually happened; then I started to read the Bible as God's written word.

I was guided through the immediate after-effects and there was a healing of local relationships. I am reminded of this every time I exchange family news with people whose lives I must have temporarily shattered. Gradually, and totally, I have been changed in attitudes, especially in relating to others.

Internal voices are associated with mental illnesses, especially schizophrenia. For those with that sad condition these voices are frequent, threatening and potentially damaging to the sufferer and others. I only heard one slowly-formed, distant word: 'Jesus'. It changed me then and continues to change me now.

Once home, in those early weeks, I had the only dream message from God that I've ever had. I dreamt about the wise rather elderly priest who had christened my son and realized I had to go and make a full confession to him. I had got myself into some really difficult and delicate situations in the run up to my conversion. The priest had become the warden of a retreat centre and I duly visited that wise old man who I now know has been a pivotal spiritual leader in our area although I certainly didn't realize that at the time. He was the right man to see. As I left the retreat centre I saw a fairly new neighbour who we thought belonged to some strange sect arriving. He and his wife proved to be Christians – living literally at the bottom of the garden. Through contact with him, and a close colleague of his, I eventually joined an active charismatic evangelical church and the rest is another story.

A note of reality: when I was converted, and for a long time afterwards, I thought all life's problems would be quickly solved by God. They were not. After three years I suddenly ended up back in hospital again and it was like the 'dark night of the soul' but this time there were Christian patients on the ward. One patient, herself a nurse, wrote out the 'Footprints' story and that has been the true reality for me.

There were other hospitalizations for the same illness and physical problems, a threat of early retirement with a young family, a car crash and many more major difficulties, but through this walk with Jesus I have been supported by him and all the friends he has brought me. I have been brought out of myself and found the truth for my life. He is truly the Way, the Truth and the Life. That first encounter was for real, it was not a delusion.

* * *

Dr Mike Hutchinson *is a consultant haematologist who for many years headed up the prayer ministry team at Holy Trinity, Leicester. He has been involved in a number of missions overseas, served in an overseas missionary hospital and speaks for ReSource[1] about healing.*

In 2006 I was sixty-six, but have two birthdays, like the Queen! In 1958 Jesus met me as I went to my home church, desperate because of a break-up with a girlfriend, and worried about my sick mother. I had been brought up by Christian parents, attended church twice on Sunday, taught in the Sunday school, passed Scripture exams and been baptized by full immersion.

While away at university in my second term I had learnt

that Mother was in hospital; but worse than that, my first love had given me the push as I lingered sixty miles distant from her. That weekend in February I journeyed home and visited Mum. Sunday came and I knew I might well meet the ex-girlfriend and her new amour at the local church. In desperation I cried to God, 'Please enable me to go to get through this and worship you.'

As I walked through the door of that small church I felt the presence of a tall manly figure; I saw Him close enough for me to touch. Though recognizable, he was not flesh and blood. Was it an angel? No, I knew this was Christ. Inside me there burst an overwhelming feeling of joy and love. I felt as if I was apart from the rest of the congregation and my feet were several inches off the floor. Physically I felt palpitations and received tears of joy. During the whole time of the service I just praised and thanked this person who was so close. And the ex-girlfriend stayed away – she later said 'so as not to hurt me'.

Later that day I returned to university still with a sense of euphoria. Head knowledge had become heart knowledge. I greeted a fellow student whom I knew to be a lively Christian with this tale. He replied – 'That's great. Can I tell the rest of the Christian Union who have been praying for you these last three months?' I suppose I had been like Samuel, who knew about God, but did not know him personally until God spoke to him.

Life changed. It was as if the world and religion that I experienced before had been on a black and white television screen. Now everything was in glorious technicolor. Prayer became a love language and the Bible an exciting meal, a love letter from God.

I had another rebuff from a girl; but this time on my

knees, I could focus on Christ: the person whom I saw and still can visualize today. My wife Ann and I met three years later.

Ten years on, our Christian lives were dry. I believe my witness in the hospital was good but my spirit felt thirsty for more. My job was coming to an end and I sought his guidance. Imagine my disappointment when God closed a door of promotion to a prestigious university position. He opened a different door for promotion in another city and by going through it Ann and I were enriched by a refilling of the Holy Spirit. It was as if we had been the disciples in Ephesus of Acts 19 who had not heard of the person and work of the Holy Spirit. We discovered about spiritual gifts and later God brought us into prayer for healing. The supernatural became natural. This was another turning point in my life's journey.

A third encounter was during a time of prayer ministry. For many years I had felt an underlying sense of guilt for which there seemed no obvious explanation. Two Christians prayed with me. As we asked the Holy Spirit to reveal what was the cause I saw and I relived a serious car accident that occurred in 1949 – forty years previously. In that prayer room I felt and saw the crucified Christ. At last it was possible to release to him the past hurts and family ramifications caused by the accident. I received freedom from the guilt that had previously hung around me for so long.

I am trained in scientific medicine. I have often asked the question 'Were these encounters just delusions, hallucinations, a sudden rush of catecholamines, dopamine or endorphins to the brain? Is it just part of my psyche? Am I just one end of a Gaussian distribution curve? Am I a machine in a closed universe?'

It is now forty-seven years since that first encounter, yet it is as fresh as if it was yesterday and still this Jesus figure meets with me, and I with him, on a daily basis. This is my reality. These are not transient events experienced under stress. They are filled with peace and joy; love, not fear. If I am just a machine, then the master programmer is still moving the keys and modifying the software!

Looking back, he has led me on a journey and brought many people alongside me. He has moulded me and goes on changing me through circumstances. I know there will be painful and difficult times ahead but I know that I never walk alone.

Sometimes God spoke very directly about problems that people would turn up with in church. One example was when during 'listening prayer' (a time when the ministry team gather to pray and to listen to God), Trevor Hesselwood [see the earlier testimony] had a picture of a right wrist with a man's watch round it. Another person in the group had already had a word about a painful arm and Trevor's word was a confirmation. Trevor said, 'these words apply to a left-handed man.' When given out to the congregation a man aged twenty-five to thirty came forward. He worked at a computer all day, was left-handed and had repetitive strain injury (RSI) of his right wrist, on which he wore his watch. After prayer the client felt warmth in the wrist and his symptoms were rapidly relieved.

In Tanzania in 2000, I visited a very poor rural area in Katesh. A young woman came for prayer. She had been unable to breathe through her left nostril for many months. There was a large swelling inside the nose which looked like a tumour. We prayed, in the name of Jesus, for the obstruction to go. The following day, she returned full of joy. 'I can breathe again,' she said through the interpreter. When we examined her, the swelling had completely disappeared!

In Zambia I had several pictures and words as we asked the Holy Spirit to come. A feeling of unilateral head pain was confirmed by a person with migrainous visual loss that was restored instantly. Several with heart palpitations and others with stomach pains responded and their symptoms disappeared!

Blackpool Rock

Don Latham *has had many jobs in local government; most notably as Chief Executive of West Wiltshire District Council where he was temporarily suspended when acting as a whistleblower on events that had taken place prior to his appointment. Despite the fact that he had only been in position a short time, his workforce walked out to support him and Don was immediately reinstated. A trial followed and sweeping changes were made. Don is a regular speaker for Full Gospel Businessmen's Fellowship International (FGBMFI), and many people, myself included, have benefited from his gracious, yet powerful ministry. This story illustrates how one miracle can lead to a whole family being converted. (See the conversion of the jailer's family in Acts 16:34 for another example!)*

In the 1980s, FGBMFI conventions were held at the Norbreck Castle Hotel in Blackpool, UK. Well-known speakers included Charles Colson of Watergate fame; I never thought that my time would come to speak to 1,000 people in this venue – especially when the main speaker was Kenneth Copeland.

During one afternoon session I was listening to Kenneth

speak on faith and I had a problem. Not with his teaching, but the fact that the convention committee had asked me to speak that evening. I felt obliged to accept because they said that, having prayed about it, they were sure I was God's choice. I was sitting there thinking, 'How can I follow this great man without looking foolish?' When I confided in my friends, they agreed that I couldn't! It is at times like these that you pray with special urgency, when you are sufficiently desperate!

Some friends from Warminster came to see me at the end of the afternoon session, and asked if I would go with them to pray for a friend, Jean, who lived in Blackpool. They had brought her to the meeting, but she had not stayed for prayer as she had been in so much pain. I wanted time to think about what I would say in the evening so rather reluctantly agreed to go with them.

They drove me along the sunlit Blackpool promenade, my eyes captivated by the varied shades of concrete and highly coloured but wasteful electric bulbs. As we made the short journey only one thought came into my mind, over and over again: 'I want Jean to know Jesus... I want Jean to know Jesus... I want Jean to know Jesus.' This was to be a lesson in God's priorities.

We arrived at a row of neat, terraced houses, which reminded me of my own former home in Wolverhampton. After a short delay, Jean made her way to the door to let us in. She was crippled with osteoarthritis. There were four of us, plus Jean, in the small, immaculate room. Keith, a big man, stood and I sat alongside Jean on the settee.

'Jean, God has spoken to me. He wants you to come to know Jesus.'

'I would love to,' she said, 'but something stops me.'

'Can I pray for what stops you? There is a prayer which is so effective in dealing with unbelief – it even works in theological college,' I said.

'Please pray for me,' she replied. As soon as I prayed, she gasped and fell back on the settee. Now, looking straight ahead, she kept on repeating the name 'Jesus.' I discovered later that she was experiencing a vision of Jesus. At this point Keith fell flat on his face on the floor, missing a perfect collection of bone china by inches. Now I had another problem because, as she repeated the name of Jesus, she squeezed my fingers – and they were becoming white. The moment Jean had received Jesus, she was healed!

She came to the convention that night, and walked in front of everyone, without her walking sticks. This was a powerful living testimony of what God had done in order not only to bless Jean, but to get people's attention. One of her daughters came that same night and made a commitment to God.

Jean's husband was an atheist; an atheist who had real difficulties when he got home from work that day and found his wife no longer crippled, and talking about Jesus. He only resisted for a few weeks before he too responded to the love of Jesus. A year later, arriving late for the start of the convention, we were put on a table with Jean's family and one of the Christian doctors from our practice. That evening our GP led the thirteenth and final member of Jean's family to the Lord. Salvation had come to a whole family in twelve months, and it had started with Jean's healing.

Some years later I was speaking at a FGBMFI dinner on the Isle of Man and this story came to mind so I shared it as part of my testimony. A young man was very keen to speak as soon as I had finished talking and I wondered what the urgency was and why he was so keen to speak. Imagine my joy to hear that he was a member of Jean's family and wanted to confirm publicly all that I had said and that he was now in training for the Anglican ministry.

Conclusion

These five encounters illustrate the sovereign power of God. Only Dr Mike Hutchinson was seeking God in any way. The others were, in CS Lewis's great phrase, 'surprised by joy'. The effects of these dramatic conversions were far-reaching. Fred Lemon, when eventually released from Dartmoor, spent the rest of his life bearing witness to his encounter in the cell; the Muslim leader is embarking on a full-time Christian ministry which will surely bear much fruit; Peter's steadfast faith in the midst of a difficult life encourages others; Dr Mike's medical knowledge and faith for healing are an attractive combination.

I was speaking in a small village in Leicestershire when I mentioned him. A woman who was present said 'My husband was very ill in hospital, probably dying, after stem cell treatment. Dr Mike came into his room, saw some Christian cards, and asked if he could pray. The results were immediate and dramatic and he is alive and well many years later.'

Jean professed faith, with no real understanding or experience, and was immediately healed. The resulting ripple spread through her family and beyond. We need to cry out to God to stretch out his hand and to reach many more of our family and friends.

Notes

1 ReSource works for the renewal of people and churches for mission in the power of the Holy Spirit. For further information go to www.resource-arm.net

3

A Presence in Prayer; Power in Scripture

[Jonathan Edwards/Michael Cassidy/Frank Houghton/
Peter Krakenberger*/Clemency Fox*/Tim Heatley*/
Martin Cavender*/Richard Atkinson*]

PRAYER IS THE MEANS BY WHICH most people seem to experience God. For some there are dramatic answers to prayer; for many the encounter, often through silent or contemplative prayer, is much more subjective and consequently difficult to write about. Scripture speaks with great power and many of the experiences included in this book were based on, or confirmed by, words of Scripture.

The extract from the writings of Jonathan Edwards combines the power of a great text with a deep experience of God as both distant and majestic and yet personal and intimate. Frank Houghton, at a time of deep distress, hears the voice of God in prayer and communicates what he hears through the medium of poetry. Michael Cassidy records many instances of the power of prayer at a time of great change in his country, South Africa. Peter Krakenberger's growing awareness of the full riches of God; Father, Son and Holy Spirit, is crystallized in an experience received through prayer with the laying on of hands. Tim Heatley hears the voice of God while praying and is led to make a very specific prayer for the protection of his mother. Clemency Fox hears the prophet Isaiah on a tape and knows that the words are for her. Martin Cavender boldly uses the power and clarity of Scripture to deflect some old friends from a very dangerous healing path. Finally, Richard Atkinson is inspired, as many others have been through the centuries, by the social teaching of Scripture to do something effective to help the unemployed find work.

* * *

Jonathan Edwards, *the great Puritan writer whose preaching and writing greatly influenced American theology in the first half of the eighteenth century (and to some extent still does so today), writes of a deep experience in which Scripture and prayer combined to speak to him.*

The first instance that I remember of that inward, sweet delight in God and divine things that I lived much in since was on reading those words (1 Timothy 1:17) 'Now unto the King eternal, immortal, invisible the only wise God be honour and glory for ever and ever, Amen'. As I read these words there came into my soul, and was as it were diffused through it, a sense of the glory of the divine Being; a new sense, quite different from anything I ever experienced before. Never had any words of Scripture seemed to me as these words did. I thought with myself how excellent a Being that was, and how happy I should be, if I might enjoy that God, and be rapt up with him in heaven, and be as it were swallowed up in him for ever! I kept saying, and as it were singing over these words of Scripture to myself; and went to pray to God that I might enjoy him, and prayed in a manner quite different from what I used to do; with a new sort of affection. But it never came into my thought that there was anything spiritual, or of a saving nature in this. From time to time, I began to have a new kind of apprehensions and ideas about Christ, and the work of redemption, and the glorious way of salvation by him. An inward, sweet sense of these things, at times, came into my heart; and my soul was led away in pleasant views and contemplations of them. And my mind was greatly engaged to spend my time in reading and meditating on Christ, on the beauty and excellency of his person, and the lovely way of salvation by free grace in him. I found no books so delightful to me as those that treated on these subjects. Those words 'I am the Rose of Sharon, and the Lily of the valleys' (Song of Songs 2:1) used to be abundantly with me. These words seemed to me sweetly to represent the loveliness and beauty of Jesus Christ.

After this my sense of divine things gradually increased, and became more and more lively, and had more of that inward sweetness. The appearance of everything was altered; there seemed to be as it were, a calm, sweet cast, or appearance of divine glory, in almost everything. God's excellency, his wisdom, his purity and love, seemed to appear in everything: in the sun, moon, and stars; in the clouds, and blue sky; in the grass, flowers, trees; in the water, and all nature; which used to greatly fix my mind. I often used to sit and view the moon for continuance; and in the day spent much time in viewing the clouds and the sky, to behold the sweet glory of God in these things; in the mean time, singing forth with as low voice my contemplations of the Creator and Redeemer.'[1]

It is interesting to note his use of the Song of Songs. Here is a meeting point with the Catholic mystics, especially St John of the Cross, whose writings are also so steeped in Scripture, especially the Song of Songs. In their days, neither would have appreciated the tradition of the other, but today the fruit of their adoration is available to help us. Likewise, his appreciation of God in nature and his delight in Christ are common ground between the different traditions.

* * *

Bishop Frank Houghton was a missionary bishop who led the China Inland Mission at the time of the communist takeover of China in 1949.

In 1971, he came to St John's College, Nottingham, where I was studying for ordination. He was a frail old man of seventy-seven, with just one more year to live, but I shall never forget his presence or his message. It was easy to sense that we were in the presence of one of God's saints. His talk revolved around what has become for me a key verse of Scripture: 'For God did not give us a spirit of timidity, but a spirit of power, of love and of self-discipline' (2 Timothy 1:7).

I had a brief talk with him in his quiet room. I don't really remember what he said, but I do remember the godly love that emanated from him. He had the fragrance of Christ (2 Corinthians 2:14–15). He had lived through years of difficult, yet exciting missionary experience in China. Eventually, just before the war, he had become the Director General of the China Inland Mission. He experienced God's blessing in wartime China, only to see everything apparently shattered by the communist takeover. Two poems from that period speak eloquently of his personal self-discipline.[2]

When God is Silent

When God is silent for a space,
And when thick darkness veils his face,
Until I hear his voice once more,
Until I see him as of yore,
On this firm ground my feet are set –
His promise, 'I WILL NOT FORGET'.

The Thick Darkness

I thought I was walking alone
Into the darkness immense and drear.
But where it was densest, a Hand touched my own,
And a voice spoke, gentle and clear:
'Do you not think you might have known
That I should be here?
Your need is met, your way will be shown,
Be of good cheer!'

These poems, written in 1951, came to him in the most difficult year of his life. The Mission had withdrawn from China, some missionaries were in prison, and the future of the church seemed uncertain. But God spoke to him with the clarity of a vision. Thick darkness was darkness 'where God was' (Exodus 20:21; 1 Kings 8:12, Isaiah 50:10).

Out of the darkness came an extraordinary vision. Withdrawal from China didn't mean the end, but a new beginning. A word came: 'Lengthen cords! Strengthen stakes!' While emphasizing the need for continuing prayer for China, the conference became convinced that they should explore new mission fields from Japan to Thailand.

For Frank, it meant the shattering experience of giving up the leadership and seeing the China Inland Mission become the Overseas Missionary Fellowship. But over the last fifty years, the power of the Lord has been seen greatly in many Asian churches – notably in Singapore and Hong Kong. In China, we hear great reports of revivals, the indigenous churches apparently flourish, despite, or perhaps because of, great persecution.

I left Bishop Houghton's old and frail presence, just beginning to understand something of the amazing power and presence of God in prayer. His testimony to God's guidance in darkness was something that all of us need to hear. Having just emerged from a period of devastation; his words and his presence were just what I needed to hear and experience.

*   *   *

Michael Cassidy, *writing about the tense days in South Africa before the 1994 elections, recounts a number of remarkable encounters with the living God. His own prayer initiatives brought many people of different races and theological understanding together. Here are two accounts of God's initiative taken as a believing man prayed:*

Colonel Johan Botha, a Christian, who after witnessing the appalling riots in Soweto in June 1976 had turned to God with even deeper intercession, was praying (unusually, for him) in English.

He said, 'God, what is it that you want for us, and what do you want for South Africa?' Immediately, he saw an angel, bathed in a brilliant indescribable light which hid his face. The angel said, 'I want South Africa on its knees in prayer.' Then the angel instructed him the need for chains of prayer services, stressed that he had fourteen days and told him 'Go to the highest authority if it is necessary.' Johan was overwhelmed and almost struck dumb with the awesome presence. But how could he take the message to the whole country? He would be laughed out of court. He made excuses, saying, 'I shall cry if I have to recount what is happening to me now'. The angel replied, 'What are a few tears compared to rivers of blood, my son?'

After the angel left, Johan wrestled in prayer for several hours. When he realized that fourteen days later was 6 April, which was Founder's Day in South Africa, Johan decided that he was prepared to go to any lengths to share the angel's message. He took his story to President de Clerk, who took his account seriously and encouraged him to call for more prayer, especially on Founder's Day. His testimony gave great impetus to a Day of National Prayer which even the newspapers regarded as a crucial factor in the peaceful outcome of the elections.

Meanwhile, the date of the election was fixed, but chaos threatened. Chief Buthelezi, Chief Minister of Kwazulu, was refusing to participate. Without his party, the elections would seem incomplete. An international team of mediators had failed. Professor Washington Okumu, a senior Kenyan diplomat, was left to pick up the pieces. He made a final attempt to contact the chief at Lanseria airport. When he arrived the chief's plane had already taken off. But something very strange happened. These are Buthelezi's own words:

We were hardly airborne when the pilot said that there was something wrong with the plane. The compass was playing up. And this was a brand new plane! So we had to return to Lanseria. Okumu had just arrived. I said to him, 'You know, my brother, God has brought me back, like Jonah, because there is something wrong with the plane, and it is obvious he wants us to meet'.

Washington Okumu then told me of a plan over which he had reflected very deeply during the night. He proposed to talk to Mr de Clerk, Mr Mandela and me to find out whether we could still discuss how to make changes in such a way that I would be able to participate in the elections. We talked at length and decided to see each other on Sunday on our way to the Jesus Peace Rally.

The conversation turned out to be a momentous turning point. Was it just a happy coincidence which led to the plane being turned back? It seems unlikely: First, the instruments had been properly checked just before take-off; secondly, if they had gone wrong a few minutes later the plane would have been diverted to a different airport; thirdly, when the plane was grounded, no errors in the compass system were found!

The Jesus peace rally was acknowledged, even in the secular press, to have played a crucial part in the whole sequence of events. It, too, had been given a very special spiritual impetus.

Such days of prayer have restarted in South Africa, mainly praying for community transformation and a revival of Spirit-led Christianity. By 2006 their influence had spread into many other African countries and even to the much more secular climate in Europe[3].

Guidance from Nature

Moses sees a burning bush; Jeremiah sees an almond twig budding; Jesus uses the unproductive fig tree to teach his disciples a powerful lesson about faith.

In the summer of 1975, recently married, Jane and I attended a Fountain Trust conference in Brighton. My expectation of experiencing God's presence and guidance, which had somewhat lapsed since my call to ordination (see the introduction), was somewhat revived.

A few weeks later, I was having a time of quiet prayer. I was sitting on the edge of a small campsite in Austria. Next to the campsite, there was a sloping field of newly cut corn which was neatly arranged in old-fashioned stooks. Along the lowest part of the field, nearest to me, were two lines of stooks – about thirty in all; up the right-hand side of the field, there were two rows of stooks which disappeared over the brow of the hill.

I was praying about a forthcoming mission in the school. I had managed to invite my old friend and mentor, Keith de Berry, to speak to the school in October, who had recently retired after a very successful ministry in St Aldates, Oxford. He had visited once before, a few years earlier. Many boys had listened with interest but we had not been organized to follow up his visit effectively. This time, I hoped that things would be different. On the previous occasion, I had not been ordained and had been kept on the periphery; now as a chaplain the organization was in my hands.

Jesus often used harvest as an evangelistic illustration. As I prayed, I sensed the Lord speaking to me about the field: 'The stooks at the bottom of the field represent boys who will be converted during the mission; the stooks up the right-hand side of the field represent the ongoing work in the school which will continue for a number of years.'

I was overwhelmed. Things had improved recently, and a young man called Roger Simpson (now vicar of St Michael le Belfry in York) had moved to Winchester and done some effective evangelism with a small number of scholars. Even so, the Christian group in the school numbered scarcely twenty to thirty new Christians. Was it possible? My young colleague Peter Krakenberger and I prayed enthusiastically for the whole school by name.

The mission started inauspiciously. Keith was given an hour to address the senior school, who were fairly unenthusiastic. Then with his high-pitched squeaky voice he told a terrible joke: 'A man went to the lunatic asylum. He asked the lunatics, "Why are you lot all here?" Quick as a flash the answer came back "Because we're not all there!"' The most intellectual school in England fell about laughing. Keith could do no wrong. Over 200 boys came voluntarily to each of his three talks. Many enquired about commitment; about thirty were converted and joined the Christian group.

The work continued. Later that term, Richard Harvey, from his liberal Jewish background (see chapter 1) was converted; a few years later (long after I had left and the group was in Peter's capable hands) so was Andrew Watson (see chapter 7).

Mark Stibbe, now vicar of St Andrew's Chorleywood and a well known author and conference speaker, writes about his experience[4]:

Peter Krakenberger encouraged the boys to meet in groups in their different houses to read the Bible, to get right with God and to pray for unsaved friends. In 1976, I became aware of the presence of Christians in my boarding house. I was severely aggravated by this, and from time to time would disrupt prayer meetings and bully those I knew who were committed Christians.

However, on 17 January 1977, I was walking down the high street in the town late at night. I remember looking up at the stars and asking, 'Is there anybody out there?' Straight away, my heart started to beat very fast as I listened to an inner voice asking the question, 'If you died tonight, where would you stand before the judgment seat of Christ?' As I considered the question, I realized that I would have absolutely no grounds for going to heaven. I had led a rebellious and sinful life. I had never accepted the call to follow Jesus Christ, though I had heard it several times before that night.

I ran as fast as I could to Peter's house. He kindly let me in even though I knew he found me a very difficult pupil. That night, however, I knelt and asked Jesus Christ to forgive me for my sins and to come into my life as my lord, my saviour and my friend.

Mark also commented that two years later, one employee of the school remarked that he had never known the atmosphere in the school be happier in fifty years. Mark's own discipleship went through a difficult period when he was first at university. But God had his hand on him. One school holiday, he had an angelic visitation in his bedroom in Norwich Cathedral Close[5].

The revival lasted about seven years. During that period it was common for a hundred boys to attend the voluntary weekly meeting of Christian Forum. It all fell apart when an influential Christian from outside the school started to

influence the group with disastrous practices and consequences. The group dwindled almost overnight to nothing,
and Peter was left to valiantly keep the flag flying in a very
hostile atmosphere. Here is his testimony of how God
renewed him some years later.

Knowing God

Peter Krakenberger *has spent his working life teaching
Mathematics at Winchester College. Shortly after he arrived,
a remarkable revival took place within the school (see also
Andrew Watson's testimony in chapter 7, and Richard
Harvey's testimony in chapter 1). Peter took over the running
of the Christian Forum soon afterwards, organized many
Bible Study groups in different houses, and for about seven
years saw a very fruitful period of ministry. After the revival
ceased, Peter ministered faithfully to the much smaller number of openly professing Christians; recently as a layman, he
has had the joy of being appointed a school chaplain.*

Ever since I can remember, I understood that it was important to know God. I was taught this both at infant school and
thereafter, and it was a truth that lodged deep in my heart.
Knowing God was the one thing that you could really boast
about (Jeremiah 9:23–24). Jesus had taught his disciples that
eternal life consisted of knowing God (John 17:3). So I
embarked on the lifelong adventure of getting to know my
maker.

I was brought up in Peru as a Roman Catholic. I took my
Catholic faith seriously, and I still remember some good
times when God seemed to draw close to me. He was my

Father who created me just as I was – timid, solitary and thoughtful. I prayed to him each day using the prayer that Jesus had taught his disciples, 'Our Father'.

But there was a problem. God was radiantly good and dazzlingly pure, and I was not. I coveted, I stole and I lied, and he said that I was not to do any of these things. My conscience troubled me and I knew that I was guilty. The years passed and I went to boarding school in England, and the problem became worse. I still went to Mass every Sunday and confessed my sins most Saturdays, but I became more and more aware of my selfishness and my basic indifference towards God.

In a flash of insight, I realized that even my good actions were selfish. I did them in order to be seen to be good or to ingratiate myself with God. Could there be any escape from the prison of my own self-centredness? I felt increasingly without hope in my longing to be right with God.

In my first term as an undergraduate at Cambridge, I was very impressed with the Christians from the Christian Union. They had a joyful and peace-filled relationship with God which I lacked. As I began to meet with them once a week, I realized that the great secret of forgiveness and being right with God was to be found in knowing Jesus Christ.

In 1968, two days after my eighteenth birthday, I asked Christ into my life and straight away I found forgiveness. There followed a deep inner peace and, in due course, joy and a longing, which I had never felt before, to share my faith.

I became associated with a group of evangelicals who worked in the public schools. Slowly but surely, my identity and my aspirations shifted from being in Jesus Christ to being part of this particular organization, I began to lose my joy and my serenity, and to imitate senior members of the organization in their sectarian and manipulative tendencies.

I still had occasional seasons of delighting in Christ, which were spiritually refreshing, but increasingly my Christian work became a dry and unfruitful experience. I suspected that other Christian groups might hold the answer for me, but the people I was with were firm in their teaching. They were confident that their approach was the right one, and they were also critical of those who had a different one. In another flash of insight, I realized that I saw any differently-minded Christians as a threat.

In particular, I had been taught to mistrust Christians who were associated with the renewal movement. But over the years, my experience was that they were beautifully loving people with a radiant faith in God. In 1995, I felt so dry that I said 'yes' when some kind friends offered to pray for me, with the laying on of hands, that I might be filled with the Spirit.

As they prayed, I felt a warmth entering my body; I had a strong sense that all was well and that God would take care of my problems. A few days later, I experienced times during which I quaked as God poured his love into my heart by the Holy Spirit. I learnt how to praise God in the Spirit; I also received a new love for certain people who had been opposing me for several years. I was able to release them into God's hands in forgiveness.

For some years there were intense difficulties, but I had a deep assurance that God would work for good in the situation that I was in. And, in due course, he did work it out in an extraordinary way: the parties who had opposed my work had to leave the school that I was working in, and I found myself vindicated and publicly commended for my stance on spiritual matters. Suddenly things changed radically for me: from being spiritually oppressed to being given freedom and encouragement in my ministry.

I have learnt that knowing God is the key to a fulfilled life. We can know him as the loving Father who created us, and who placed us in a beautiful world full of opportunities. We can know him as our self-giving saviour who redeemed us, and who gave us a new start to a life of purposeful service. Otherwise we would have wandered even further astray along the path that leads to destruction. And we can know him as our strengthening sanctifier who provides us with love and the dynamic power to lead holy lives that are pleasing to God. We can know the God who is the one true God but who is also three persons. Because he is plural he can be love, and to know him in his plurality is a varied and enriching experience (see especially Jeremiah 9:23–24; John 17:3; Romans 5:5).

* * *

Tim Heatley *was an accountant working in industry before contracting severe glandular fever which progressed to ME. As he was unable to continue working, he took early retirement. He now uses his time to help run a group within the East Midlands for ME sufferers. Before his illness, he used to be a youth leader and enjoyed organizing sporting activities for young Christians. Now he is very involved in prayer and enjoys communicating Christian happenings to his circle of friends.*

About ten years ago, we as a family experienced some very important divine help. I was going to bed when I heard the

Holy Spirit whisper to me 'Pray for angels to guard your mum tonight'. I thought this was a bit bizarre and doubted the guidance. To me, angels were a bit in the same context as fairies and goblins. I am macho and not into that sort of thing.

So I delayed. However, the voice came again: 'Pray for angels to guard your mum tonight.' My rational thinking was that my mum, who is elderly, would go to bed, go to sleep and wake up in the morning unharmed. What dangers could there be? The doors were locked; I was on hand in case of any attempted break-in or fire. This did not make sense.

However, I thought 'What have I got to lose?' So I prayed for angels to keep guard over my mum that night. I thought no more about it and went to bed and to sleep.

The next morning I got up to have breakfast and had quite frankly forgotten about the experience the night before. But then I was suddenly jolted into a sense of reality when my mum began to speak. She said that during the night she had decided she needed to go downstairs for something (some medicine I think) but as she got to the top of the stairs, she tripped and fell the full length of the stairs. As she reached the bottom, she found herself being caught up into the arms of angels and being gently lowered to the ground. She got up without a scratch or bruise. Although she did not see the angels, she felt them holding her.

This was a very sobering experience and has taught me to listen more closely to the promptings of the Holy Spirit. Psalm 34:7 'The angel of the Lord encamps around those who fear him' would seem an appropriate text!

A Checkered Career

Clemency Fox *has been involved with Christian work in a variety of ways; here she tells how God spoke to her through Scripture and how he sustained her through two marriages – the first of which ended in divorce and the second with bereavement.*

One day in 2003 I was driving through Headington, Oxford – I remember it clearly – with a CD playing in the car that I had listened to many times before. Suddenly I heard, as if for the first time, a voice reading these words from Isaiah 54:

'Do not be afraid; you will not suffer shame.
Do not fear disgrace; you will not be humiliated.
You will forget the shame of your youth
and remember no more the reproach of your widowhood.

For your Maker is your husband –
the Lord Almighty is his name –
the Holy One of Israel is your Redeemer;
he is called the God of all the earth.

The Lord will call you back
as if you were a wife deserted and distressed in spirit –
a wife who married young,
only to be rejected,' says your God.

'For a brief moment I abandoned you,
but with deep compassion
I will bring you back.

> In a surge of anger
> I hid my face from you for a moment,
> but with everlasting kindness
> I will have compassion on you,'
> says the Lord your Redeemer.

I heard this as if the Lord, the Holy Spirit, was speaking to me personally! This word came into my life at precisely the moment when I could receive it; I believe that this was God communicating directly with me through his Word.

As the subtitle above indicates, my life has been anything but straightforward. I was married in 1959, the year I left university, and just over a year after that my husband began acting unfaithfully – sleeping with a woman who worked in the same organization. Because his job at that time demanded nights and weekends away from home he was thrown into the company of colleagues. He saw more of them than he did of me, so it was easy. Over the next year or so we made various attempts to make our marriage work (we were both Christians), but he gave up in the end because he wanted to be with his girlfriend, and started asking me to divorce him. Eventually I did, and this happened four years after we were married.

I was twenty-six years old, 'a wife who married young, only to be rejected...' And certainly, I was 'deserted and distressed in spirit'. It was a time of huge grief and shame, and the distress was overwhelming. I felt neglected, abandoned, unloved, unworthy. But I think the worst of all those feelings was that I believed that I was unlovable. But I am so grateful to God for my family and friends, especially Christian friends, who were supportive and caring.

Very, very slowly and with many stumbles, I began to

build a new life. For ten years I lived a single life in London, working in various jobs – some interesting, some not so interesting. At this stage in my life I felt myself to be quite remote from God but not completely cut off. It was as if he had me attached to him by a very stretchy piece of elastic. I did not belong to any Christian fellowship, went to church spasmodically if at all, but continued to spend time with Christian friends, some of whom I know were praying for me.

Then I met the next man in my life and after some years, and quite a few doubts and uncertainties, we married and made our home on the outskirts of Oxford. He was the nicest man I ever met and we had nineteen years of marriage. Through our love for one another and the fellowship of the local parish church as well as through much reading and study, I gradually re-emerged into an active Christian faith.

When my husband died I was bereft once more, experiencing overwhelming desolation and abandonment – 'the reproach of widowhood'. But I know now that God had never taken his hand off me, and over a number of years I lived through the grief and suffering of bereavement, until it eventually came to an end. During those years I received incredible love and support from the Christian fellowship of my parish church. God gave me work to do, which I could not have done easily had I still been married.

Moreover, I really cannot thank God enough for loving prayer and wise counsel from many people, but especially from a Christian couple who are now close and much loved friends, from my sisters in Christ in the Lydia Fellowship and also from the Harnhill Centre for Christian Healing, where, several times, I have experienced the Lord's healing touch in a way that I cannot easily put into words. Then, at the right moment, he guided me, step by step, into moving from the home where I had lived for thirty-one years into a totally new place, new friends and neighbours, new Christian fellowship, new challenges and commitments. I know that this is all of his choosing.

Now, fourteen years after my husband's death, my experience is of huge and seemingly continuous blessing. I have come to know the Lord in a fresh and exciting way and to know that I am loved 'beyond understanding'. God has given me a love of Scripture which is a precious gift and an understanding that the gift of himself is the greatest gift of all. I am so thankful.

> For your Maker is your husband –
> the Lord Almighty is his name –
> the Holy One of Israel is your Redeemer;
> he is called the God of all the earth.

*   *   *

Martin Cavender *was for many years an ecclesiastical lawyer, Diocesan Registrar for Bath and Wells; he was then called by Archbishops George Carey and John Hapgood to direct and administer 'Springboard', their new initiative on Evangelism. He organized, and taught for this important work from 1992 to 2004. He is now director of ReSource, which brings together the renewal work of Anglican Renewal Ministries with the mission experience of Springboard, and he speaks and teaches around the UK and overseas. He is supported in all this by his wife Cesca who is also part of the prayer ministry team at Harnhill Christian Healing Centre, near Cirencester. In this encounter, the power of Scripture to teach, rebuke and correct (2 Timothy 3:16) is very apparent!*

The Pendulum and the Black Box

When I was working in Somerset I formed a friendship with a churchwarden from a little rural church, and his wife – I'll call them David and Mary. He had been a soldier with a distinguished Second World War record as an officer in a fine Regiment, and was now retired. They lived in a small cottage in their village.

Our friendship developed, and the two or three of us began to meet for a simple lunch on a reasonably regular basis. We would talk over all sorts of things, shared interests; but we always included a high proportion of faith questions, and often got down to reading passages from the Bible together.

Mary had a wasting disease which medical science seemed unable to explain or touch, and which meant that she was virtually blind and in constant pain. One day David and Mary arrived for lunch as agreed, and Mary came in looking better than I had ever seen her, with her eyes open and bright. They were watching to see if I would notice that something had happened. It was clearly a transformation, and I said so. What had happened? Mary told me she had been healed, prayed for by a member of their congregation. It was all very exciting, and I asked for details over the lunch.

Mary told me this woman had prayed for her 'using a pendulum which she swung over a black box'. My spirit began trembling. David was watching me carefully. I didn't quite know what to say, so asked if the woman had used the name of God, or of Jesus, or had invited the Holy Spirit in her prayers? No she had not. The atmosphere was getting distinctly apprehensive, but I felt I had to press on. David was clearly getting irritated with me, and Mary was looking increasingly unhappy.

'Do you know of any pendulum or black box in Scripture?' I asked, with a growing sense of unease. 'No,' said Mary. I said something haltingly about other spirits and counterfeits, about freedom and bondage, and then asked, 'Would you want anything to do with this healing if it were not of Jesus?' After a long silence, Mary replied, 'No, I would not,' looking more and more fearful. We were driving into something from which I couldn't reverse, and by this time David was obviously very angry. Mary was clearly in better health than she had been for years and here I was questioning it and frightening her. It was touch and go whether he would whisk her away. Our friendship was in serious jeopardy.

It occurred to me to open the Bible, picking up the only clear passage I knew on this subject – James 5:14–16. We read it together. I explained that I only knew of one kind of healing, in the name of Jesus in the power of the Holy Spirit – and this was what James was talking about.

Casting about frantically for inspiration I suggested that if Mary really didn't want anything to do with this healing then she could pray, with David, and renounce it in the name of Jesus. If it had been a Godly happening, there would be no problem. If not? Well, it occurred to me in my naïve understanding to warn her that there might be side-effects – if she decided to renounce the 'healing' and it was not of God she could well find that her sight would go, and the pain might return. It seemed right to say all this, but I didn't really know what I was talking about. I was quite a young Christian believer, and I was flying by the seat of my pants.

I also said that if all that happened, then they should immediately contact their local parish priest (a young man who had been in post only, I think, for a few weeks), and ask him to pray for Mary's healing. The passage from James might be a useful text. Lunch ended. They left – and I was really not sure if they would ever want to see me again. Chastened but increasingly clear about what had been happening, I went back to my office. I prayed.

Three weeks later, I had a phone call. It was David. 'Do you fancy some lunch?' 'Yes!' I almost shouted in my relief. We fixed up a date.

The day arrived, and so did David and Mary. She was looking radiant, and they were both grinning at me. 'OK, come on, what's happened?' I asked. The story came out.

They had gone home from the previous lunch angry (David) and confused and fearful (Mary). They had thought and talked about what had been said, and then after ten days decided they couldn't put it off any more. They had knelt together beside their bed, and together renounced anything in this 'healing' which was not of Jesus Christ. Instantly Mary's sight went, and her pain returned, worse than ever. It was a very frightening moment.

David went straight to the phone and rang the vicar. 'I want you to come round and pray with us for my wife to be healed.' The vicar explained that he had no experience of the healing ministry. 'That's all right,' said David, 'James will tell us what to do. See you in the church in ten minutes, Vicar.'

I thank God for that young parish priest. Despite his lack of experience he turned up on parade in the church at the prescribed time, knelt on one side of the altar rail with Mary on the other, read aloud the passage from James, and did what it said in the book. He prayed for Mary to be healed, and anointed her with oil. And Mary was healed, wholly and completely, of her sight problems and all her pain, in the name of Jesus, in the power of the Holy Spirit, there and then.

Mary lived on in her healing for another four years, and then died peacefully in a hospital bed. There was more healing going on than just the physical on that day in Somerset, however.

David and Mary discovered afresh the God of power who loved them. The vicar found a new ministry which was clear and undeniable. I learned so much, in all my awkwardness, and again saw a loving God at work among his people – and I learned that it was vital to speak out, whatever the social or personal risk. My only sadness was that I didn't think more about that woman in the congregation whose offering of healing by the pendulum and the black box had precipitated the whole thing. I can only pray that someone somewhere has helped her see the truth, and helped her recognize that the evil one 'masquerades as the angel of light' (2 Corinthians 11:14). I know that my job as a believer is to stand in the name of Christ and ask, 'By what spirit?'

A Church Porch in 1995

The Venerable Richard Atkinson OBE *has served as parish priest in Sheffield and Rotherham. In both places, part of his witness to the gospel was extensive community engagement including projects responding to youth and adult unemployment – very serious social issues in these urban priority area parishes. Since 2002, he has served as Archdeacon of Leicester.*

'But let justice roll down like waters, and righteousness like an ever-flowing stream' (Amos 5:24, NASB).

'Why do you bother with us?'

I was used to questions from the lads and occasional lass who gathered under the inviting porch of our church on the Manor estate, Sheffield. Branded in the media as the worst estate in Britain (some years earlier we had also been credited with the worst pub in Britain) the usual comments reflected the concerns and issues of the increasingly alienated young people. There was anger at the perceived favoured status of Somalian refugees who had been housed in the area; the thrill of joyriding; the boredom of their lives and the lack of provision for them; a roll-call of who was absent as a guest of her majesty; and all the time a dismissal of the church. I learnt to let the constant foul language, aggressive tone and comment wash over me.

For several years I spent evening after evening from about 10.00 p.m. onwards standing with these lads – partly, to be honest, to try and protect the church from damage, but also very much as an expression of Christian love and concern.

From time to time slightly deeper questions would be asked. We would discuss for a while issues in their lives or in the world, before inevitably someone would lose interest and the banality would start again. And then one of the lads asked, 'Why do you bother with us?'

I can't remember all that I said, but I spoke of my belief that before God each and every person was precious; that there was something of the image of Jesus Christ in each of us; that I believed they were of significance; that God loved them.

At one level nothing dramatically changed. Cars were still regularly stolen and set on fire. The youth centre was burnt down and the building next to the vicarage was also set on fire – after eight years on the estate my antennae were finely tuned and I knew that this would happen that evening, but you can't call the fire brigade and say 'I am ringing to tell you about a fire which hasn't yet happened!' The lads continued to gather and the damage and nuisance carried on.

Yet things did change after that encounter.

Later that year the church was seriously damaged – every window in our precious new church centre was attacked with a screw-driver. It was symbolic of the wider nuisance on that part of the estate and because it coincided with a national report on disaffected youth I found myself on the front page of the Daily Telegraph. Indeed for three days the press camped around us as the estate received its 'worst estate' tag and we were news. A few days later, after the story had died, we gathered people in the church with our MP to try and build new hope for the future. In the room were many angry older people – most of them had experienced incessant nuisance – and there were also many of the lads and some of the lasses. They were there because trust had grown between us, but they weren't there for long! A few angry comments about 'the youth' and they were off. With a glance to the MP whom I knew well I left to find them and after some time was able to bring them back in. I don't know exactly what they felt, but there was a recognition that they were being 'bothered with'.

From that meeting various things happened. One of the most profound experiences for me was that following my appearance in the national press people, mainly other Christians, sent me money – it was a truly moving experience to discover that Christians across the country who didn't know me still wanted to show their support. A church in Jersey even invited us as a family over for a week's holiday – a deeply moving expression of Christ's love. I too was learning what it meant to be loved and valued. The money itself allowed us to employ a worker and before long 'Manor Reborn' was established to offer IT training and other support to these lads.

Equally memorable was a walk on the moors where a number of the lads were joined by the local police officers, the Chief Constable, the MP and myself.

'Why do you bother with us?' That encounter with one young man was another stage on my journey of encounter with the living God who is present in his creation and who seeks not just the transformation of individual lives but the renewal of society as his kingdom is built, not just in heaven but here on earth. The prophet Amos's words of challenge to the indulgent, errant and unjust people of Israel, 'But let justice roll down like waters, and righteousness like an ever flowing stream' (Amos 5:24 NASB) guided me then and have inspired me ever since as I have tried to enable, albeit in a very modest way, that divine love and justice to be present in our world; as I have sought to follow a calling that has been very much about ministry in the world.

In Rotherham, where I moved next to be vicar of the town centre parish church, it included representing the churches on the strategic partnership and chairing a partnership company which made significant inroads into unemployment in the town. In Leicester the challenge of justice and righteousness has included the call to be the independent chair of a £50 million New Deal for Communities regeneration scheme which has travelled from near disaster to making a significant impact on the area. God's justice and righteousness very much still need to flow throughout our land.

The encounter was also part of a journey for the young man who asked the question. In time he was to take a lead in the foundation of 'Manor Reborn'; subsequently he would become a trainer of others; and only last month I heard of how over the years he too had 'bothered' with many other young people in the area.

The church porch at St Swithun's was in many ways a huge mistake. Designed as an expression of welcome it quickly became a place of nuisance and damage; most of the time I wished that we had never built it. Indeed, I would caution others, who are designing new churches or extensions, to be wary of such places where groups can gather. Yet it was a place of deep encounter, not just with young men and women but with the presence and love of God in action. Again and again over the years I have known both the challenge and the power of the God who in his desire that all may have life and have it abundantly, wishes that his justice and righteousness might flow through the world.

Manor didn't deserve the 'worst estate' tag. Although it had its tough times – another part of the estate was paralleled to war-torn Beirut because of the scale of threat and damage – it was a place of special people and some of the best community projects in the country, which of themselves were outworkings of justice and righteousness.

'Why do you bother with us?' Whoever you are, the answer is quite simply because you are special; you are my neighbour; God loves you.

Conclusion

It would be difficult to find two more contrasting stories than the last two – yet in each case the encounters were underpinned by a knowledge and application of Scripture. In one case, a dangerous spiritual remedy was reversed; in the other, a great project which touched many young people was inspired.

All these testimonies are just the tiniest tip of a very large iceberg. One thing is certain: if we don't make time to pray and read the Scriptures, we will greatly reduce the likelihood that God will speak to us directly. When we pray, and when we read the Scriptures with an open heart, we seem to open a channel for an encounter with the living God.

Notes

1 Iain H. Murray, *Jonathan Edwards, Banner of Truth*, 1987, page 35.
2 Frank Houghton, *Faith Triumphant*, OMF Books, 1973, pages 131–32.
3 Michael Cassidy, *A Witness for Ever*, Hodder and Stoughton, 1995, pages 160 and 163.
4 Mark Stibbe, *Thinking Clearly about Revival*, Monarch, 1998, page 24.
5 John Woolmer, *Angels of Glory and Darkness*, Monarch, 2006, page 30.

4

Visions, Dreams and Signs

[Elizabeth Brazell*/Daniel Cozens*/Kenneth McAll/
Demos Shakharian]

MANY OF US STRUGGLE with the whole question of guidance. Often the way forward seems unclear and we have to take a decision trusting that God will block it if we are stepping outside his will. Sometimes God speaks so decisively that our questions are answered once and for all time! I have recorded one such occasion in my own life at the end of this chapter; here are some other examples of God intervening decisively in people's lives. In each case, the communication is wonderfully detailed – the name of a house, a powerful and personal dream; an exact sum of money; angelic protection and a prophecy given to an illiterate boy which was used many years later to protect a group of Christians from a terrible massacre.

Finding the House of Bread

Elizabeth Brazell *was ordained in 1987, working alongside her husband Denis in Reading. Subsequently, she has worked for Springboard (the evangelism initiative of the Archbishops of Canterbury and York) and has founded the Word for Life Trust which encourages mission and healing in this country and has helped a* *number of projects overseas notably in India and Kenya. Here is her account of some very dramatic guidance which led to a major change of location for WFLT.*

The Word for Life Trust came into being in the mid-1990s as a ministry of healing and evangelism working throughout the UK and overseas to train and to model this work of God. In 1994 I was working in a parish in Reading, where my husband Denis was the vicar and chair of the town's Churches Together group. That year 'Springboard', a mission initiative of the Archbishops of Canterbury and York, was invited to lead a mission to the Thames Valley. As a result of this I was invited to coordinate further missions in many other areas of the UK and overseas. Since being called to full time Christian ministry in 1977 I had always worked in healing, counselling, worship leading and evangelism.

In 1995 I received many invitations, from the United Kingdom and overseas, inviting me to train and lead in the areas of mission, leadership, healing, Christian counselling, prayer ministry and evangelism. The Diocese of Oxford agreed to release me from parish ministry, and a trust was set up in 1995 to give me freedom to travel and to serve full time in the areas of mission, evangelism and healing.

Initially called the Nathan Trust, this was changed when the trust applied for charity recognition. The Charity Commissioners gave the trust formal recognition as 'Word for Life' in May 1997. The trust is governed by a deed of trust, and a board of trustees meets three or four times each year to provide legal oversight of the work.

A team of leaders, administrative helpers, counsellors, pastoral carers, trainers, teachers, intercessors and evangelists has gradually formed and now works alongside myself and the other leaders. Now the core team numbers fourteen (full-time, part-time and volunteers) and there are many prayer ministry/counsellors, trainers and volunteer evangelists. The ministry now works in and from a resource and retreat centre, The House of Bread, in the Forest of Dean and continues to also serve around the United Kingdom and abroad.

On 10 January 1999, the members of the leadership team of WFLT had a day of prayer followed by a meeting when all agreed that the Lord was calling us to look for a place as a resource centre and that we were to have all things in common. A 'word' was received in the time of silence, as follows:

> My child, do not be surprised at the site of this special place. It will be called 'Bethlehem' (or the house of bread). My word is life and my son is the bread of life. It is to be a place of resource, of healing, of listening, of play, of receiving and restoration; through it my church will be blessed... Wait and see what I will do and go to look when and where I tell you.

So the hunt began. As the Word for Life Trust was working out of offices in Milford on Sea, we assumed that the building which we were to name the House of Bread would be on the south coast or in the New Forest area. But every time we got close to buying a possible hotel or similar property the sale would fall through at the last moment. In February 2002 we were still enquiring of the Lord and asking him to close the door if were going 'the wrong way'. We went on our leadership team retreat again and heard the Lord clearly say 'Look for the House of Bread' and again, 'Don't be surprised at the venue for the resource centre.'

Consequently, we widened our search and prayed again, and over the next few weeks several friends suggested suitable areas and properties. I toured the country, always with one other leader as company, looking at seven possible sites. On 19 March I arrived late in the evening at Brecon with an order to view a property on the edge of the town. We were staying overnight at the home of one of our intercessors and after a time of prayer for guidance went to bed and slept soundly until the early hours.

I awoke at about 4 a.m. after a vivid dream in which I was wandering around a building made of greyish-pink stone with a very distinctive stained glass window of creation pictures. I wrote this down and fell asleep for a while only to wake a little later, about 5 a.m., with a clear inner voice saying, 'Go to Monmouth, find the statue in the town square, go to the estate agent behind the statue, witness to me and tell them you have come to buy the House of Bread.'

I prayed and knew that our Lord had guided us clearly as he had promised. So I cancelled the order to view in Brecon and drove straight to Monmouth to look for the statue.

At 9 a.m. that same morning I was given the particulars of 'The House of Bread' in the estate agent behind the statue. I witnessed to the dream and what the Lord had said and the estate agent wanted to know every detail.

She said that the property she was selling was now called the Old Bakery but when it had originally been built in 1752 it had been called the House of Bread. It had supplied bread to the neighbourhood until 1956. The price was right, and the Lord had told us that we would have all that was needed to buy the House of Bread!

My colleague and I immediately went to view the property and there was the stone of greyish pink colour (Forest of Dean stone) and the exact stained glass window I had seen in my dream. The window was hand-made by the daughter of the current owner. This was 20 March 2002 and we moved in with all legal matters completed on 16 May – under two months later! To God be the glory. The House of Bread is now a healing and training centre and home of the Word for Life Trust and Arts in Mission offices.

The resource centre is decidedly tailor-made for us with three 'cottage homes', one each for three couples who make up the community there. There is also an office, a barn converted ready to be a teaching room/chapel and space for a bookstore, creative arts and catering – we praise God for His provision.

So where does that leave me as I reflect on the way our Lord leads and guides? Firstly again, he has underlined the immense importance of listening to him and making space to listen and enquire. Secondly, the Lord is sovereign in all circumstances and his plans and purposes are always fulfilled. Thirdly, he truly does guide us step by step and his Word is 'a lamp unto our feet and a light unto our paths'. Yes, the Lord knew our needs and had all things prepared for us to walk in. Finally, his timing is perfect.

This whole process has deepened my trust in God, the God who loves me as a perfect Father and who gave me new life in Jesus and is daily working to sanctify me by the power of his indwelling Holy Spirit. I thank him for his love and patience and as a leadership team we all have learnt much through this process especially about love and community.

I finish by paraphrasing part of Acts 16 from *The Message* by Eugene H. Peterson. 'Their plan was to turn left towards Bournemouth, but the Holy Spirit blocked that route. So they went to Southampton and tried to go north to Lyndhurst but the Spirit of Jesus wouldn't let them go there either. Proceeding on through the motorway they went to the

Brecon Beacons but the Lord sent them south again near the mouth of the Severn and Wye rivers. That night there was a dream and... all the pieces had come together!'

Do come and visit us in Macedonia (the Forest of Dean)!

*   *   *

Daniel Cozens *is a full-time evangelist. One of his best-known ventures is the 'Walk of 1,000 Men'. He also uses art to present the Christian faith. Here is his striking account of the sign that confirmed that he should set up the walks, of which there have been about ten.*

However immature looking for a sign from God can some-times appear, there are times in our lives when it seems the only way. In any case, men of God have done this, especially so in the Old Testament and there is a specific reference in Malachi when God actually encourages this. The sign that God gave me in answer to prayer changed both my ministry and me.

As an evangelist, conducting many successful missions during the 1980s, I felt the great need to go beyond the church, as stated in Hebrews 13:13. It became such a per-sistent desire in my life that I felt led to mobilize men to do more evangelism and take steps to challenge the stifling insu-larity of the church. I yearned to go beyond the town and citywide parish ministries I was conducting.

Consequently, I planned two missions, one for six weeks and one for three in the Arts Theatre, Cambridge, which is local to my home. They both took place during lunchtimes in the theatre, with the assistance of local Christians. I also set up fifteen evening meetings in different pubs in my area –

five each week for three weeks – the results of which were hugely encouraging.

I spent a day in prayer and fasting on 11 January 1989. It was then that God laid the title and the vision of 'The Walk of 1,000 Men' on my heart. I reeled with excitement and subsequently shared this proposal with some close colleagues.

With the approval of those I trusted I sought a wider response. I wrote to about 600 men I knew, asking them to come to a meeting in Cambridge where I could share with them the vision: to step out in faith by going on a walking mission down the Pennines without money, wallets, or phones. As a priority, I wanted to propose that we visit the public houses twenty miles either side of the Pennines and we ask the churches in those areas to provide church-hall floors for men to sleep on whilst also encouraging their own churches to participate.

I told the men there would be a collection taken at the meeting that would help fund the vision. Prior to this meeting, I asked God for a sign. I did not share this with anyone else. I asked God that there should be exactly £10,000 in the offering. If this request was answered, I would do the walk, if not, I wouldn't – it was as simple as that. I thought this through and made the prayer. As the collection bags were circulated on the day I wondered how the Lord would answer. I was excited; my main problem now was that I wanted to do this. Judging by the response of the men they were frightened about this outreach, but even so, ready to do this 'foolish' thing for God. We sang another hymn whilst the money was counted.

Gillie my wife, along with Lynda, a secretary from the TFM office, were the only two women present, and after they had counted the money Gillie told me, with great excitement, that there was £5,500 in the collection. I turned immediately to the congregation and told them plainly that there would be no walk. Not surprisingly, they were aghast – and Gillie too was puzzled and confused, expressing the incredulity of others and asking why not? I then told her and the assembled men about my private prayer and the sign I had asked for from our most wonderful God.

As we stood there on that day I felt, with others, that it would be unwise to go against such a serious prayer.

However, before one minute had passed, my wife asked me to hold on as she had found, tucked in the corner of one of the collection bags, a piece of paper which was an IOU for £4,500 (an amount which was subsequently paid within the week) – which of course equalled the £10,000! What rejoicing there was! When the first walk took place in 1991 we visited 600 public houses and 400 churches, finishing on a rainy day in Tintwhistle. We knew by now that God had lit a tremendous fire.

* * *

Kenneth McAll *was a medical missionary in the 1930s with, amongst others, the Olympic gold medallist Eric Liddell. He and his wife were interned by the Japanese during the war. After his release, he studied psychiatry and promoted what he called 'the Healing of the Family Tree' – a ministry which released many patients and others from the effects of their ancestors' spiritual problems. I first heard him speak in Winchester Cathedral.*

It was a beautiful June afternoon. The ancient cathedral seemed strangely still. The tourists were quiet and a small congregation prepared for an unusual event – unusual in the 1970s – a service of healing in an Anglican cathedral.

The speaker was a small, seemingly elderly, man. He was in his sixties, but the ravages of wartime imprisonment by the Japanese made him look older. His high-pitched voice was quite difficult to hear. After the normal pleasantries, he launched into his talk with a personal reminiscence.

Before the Second World War, Ken McAll and his wife Frances had been missionaries in China. It was a threatening time, with constant danger both from the Red Army which was trying to wrest control from the nationalistic government, and from the Japanese who were also invading parts of China. Ken, Eric Liddell and other mission workers were increasingly aware of God's direction, and protection.

Ken explained that one day, he was returning to Siaochang along the rough road through the fields and heading towards the village, when he was aware of someone walking behind him. He was told not go to that village, but to go instead to a different village, where he was needed. Ken took it to be the voice of a local farmer who knew what was going on. It was best not to show any fear by looking round.

When he reached the village, the gate was opened, and he was pulled inside. The villagers asked him what had made him change direction (some of them had watched him from afar). Ken said 'That man out there told me to come,' but when he, and the locals, looked out there was no one else to be seen. Then Ken realized that his unseen companion had spoken in English – unlikely for a Chinese farmer!

The villagers then told him that if he had continued in the direction that he was heading, he would have landed in a Japanese trap, as the village to which he had been walking was occupied by Japanese troops. Moreover, a local skirmish had left several wounded, some of whom had been brought into the village, and several people needed his medical attention. One of the wounded became a Christian, and eventually joined the staff of the teacher training college where Eric Liddell had taught.

Ken knew that his life had been saved by the direct intervention of the Lord. His worldview had changed. Writing about the incident he commented, 'My mocking intolerance of the implicit belief of the Chinese in ghosts and the spirit world was gone. I understood, too, that the spirit world holds both good and evil influences, and I realized that my daily prayer for protection had been dramatically answered.'

This was the highly unusual beginning to a very challenging talk. Ken continued with an account of his wartime captivity, shared with his wife, during which they had discovered that the power of prayer could replace unavailable medicines. As prisoners, they had been crammed into a freezing cold factory, into which some 1,200 prisoners had been herded by the Japanese.

The talk then moved on to tell of his more recent experiences of healing, including new insights into psychiatry which he had gained during post-war studies. He spoke as though the sort of experiences that he was relating should be part of our normal Christian life.

This was the first time that I had heard anyone talk about angelic encounters. The New Testament came alive in a new way and my worldview was somewhat changed. These sort of visionary encounters are a very powerful witness to God's presence in our troubled world. Here is an example from a hundred years ago which still influences people today!

The Happiest People on Earth

Demos Shakarian *founded the Full Gospel Businessmen's Fellowship International; this organization has influenced many people and transformed many people's lives and businesses. None of this would have come to pass if his grandfather hadn't been guided to leave Kara Kala in Turkish Armenia.[1]*

In about 1850, a lad called Efim who couldn't read or write heard the Lord calling him into another long prayer vigil. On the seventh day, he received a vision which he laboriously copied; writing down the shapes and forms that had passed before his eyes. His diagrams and letters were taken to people in the village who could read. The results were dramatic!

At some future, unspecified time, every Christian in Kara Kala would be in great danger. They must flee and the boy drew a map. The map was unmistakably of the Atlantic Ocean and the east coast of America! The written instructions were that they would be told when to leave and that, when they crossed the Atlantic, they were not to settle there, but to cross the continent and settle on the opposite coastline.

Demos' grandfather had had some prophetic experiences – one concerning the exact date of the birth of his son and one uncomfortable one when he had served up a blind and flawed steer for a feast for some visiting Russian Christians. His misdemeanour had been dramatically exposed. As a result, he was much more open to listening to Efim's prophecy.

About fifty years after the original vision, just after the turn of the twentieth century, Efim said the time had come.

'We must flee to America – all who stay will perish.' The
Christians in Kara Kala had had other prophetic experiences
and many, including Demos' grandfather, obeyed. In 1914,
after the First World War had started, the Turkish people
organized a systematic massacre of the Armenian Christians.
Very few escaped. Many were burnt to death – they were
locked in a building and given the choice of converting to
Islam or being burnt alive.

Those who had escaped to America heard the news with
awe and dismay. They had obeyed the prophecy and crossed
America and settled in Los Angeles. Many of them were living close to Azusa Street in Los Angeles where the
Pentecostal church was born in about 1908! The Armenian
refugees were involved right at the beginning. They received
much blessing from the early Pentecostals and their situation
as refugees was greatly transformed!

Many years later, again through dramatic prophecy, the
FGBMFI was formed. None of this would have happened
without the illiterate boy's prophecy some hundred years earlier.

Conclusion

Mathematically, the odds against these events occurring by
chance must be phenomenal! But when God is in charge,
amazing things have a habit of happening! Also, when God
speaks, it is wise to act; many other stories in this short book
will take up this theme. The consequences of disobedience
for the Armenian Christians would have been drastic; for the
other writers it would have been a matter of missing God's
best. If we believe that God has 'plans to prosper you and not

to harm you' (Jeremiah 29:11) then we will expect that, from time to time, he will communicate with us very directly. On other occasions, he will expect us to follow our spiritual intuition and act in faith.

Years after the Ambleside experience, I was looking for a new job. I had just turned forty and despite a lot of offers nothing really suitable had turned up. After a visit to the Bishop of Bath and Wells, I applied for the job of rector at Shepton Mallet, but was politely turned down by the patrons who were the Duchy of Cornwall.

About four weeks later, I was in great indecision. I had been offered a good job in Derby, but it didn't feel quite right; I was also on the point of being offered a very good post in Eastbourne. I had also had a really good interview, conducted in 10 Downing Street, by a retired brigadier who looked after the Crown Appointments livings. In some confusion, I went to see my friend James Haig-Ferguson who headed a Christian community at Stanton House, near Oxford. He prayed and then, very simply, said, 'Father says you will hear something significant in the next week'.

Two days later, one of the churchwardens at Shepton Mallet rang up and invited me down for an interview. Shepton Church was of a different tradition to what we were used to, and the interviews were a bit hair-raising. At one point, the curate whispered to me, 'The lady churchwarden has disagreed with everything that you've said, but keep going!' To our surprise we were offered the job.

We gathered a small group of friends to pray. There was a general, but not complete consensus as to which of the three jobs was right. Shepton Mallet was the risky choice, but it seemed to fit what we were looking for. As we prayed, our parish worker saw a picture in her mind of a long, low, grey stone building. It didn't register with me, but Jane said it was the rectory at Shepton Mallet. Indeed it was! It was the only possible description of the Elizabethan former grammar school and our parish worker, who was Canadian and had never even been to Somerset, confirmed it five months later when she came down for our induction. She stood at the entrance of the house, surveyed the long, grey stone building and gasped!

The next morning James rang up with a prophetic word: 'Choose this day where you will serve. Choose the place where as a family you all will fit most naturally. I want your roots to take hold within the whole community and not just the body of the church. For as you are accepted and become part – not merely as a minister – but as a man, a wife, a family within that same community, so shall the deep groundswell begin that will shake you as well as those you serve. Not that anyone shall be destroyed, but rather all shall find together that due measure of fulfilment in my name and in my word that is according to the need not only of each one, but of the whole community. So choose where you most naturally fit; for you will serve me there for many years.'

We certainly needed to decide that day; we had already kept the church in Derby waiting far too long. Shepton Mallet was the only community church, the other two were eclectic gathered congregations with little actual parish. We were there a long time – almost twenty years. I don't think we ever quite saw the groundswell but the church did become much more established in the community. We were shaken and changed; so was the church.

The next day, the retired brigadier who ran the Crown Appointments Board rang up to offer me a living. He was a prayerful, caring man; but his offer came one day too late. I had chosen and I wasn't going back on my God-given choice!

Note

1 Demos Shakharian, *The Happiest People on Earth*, Hodder and Stoughton, 1975, chapter 1.

5

Out of the Jaws of Death

[Ian McCormack/Randy Vickers*/David Ridge*/James Charles*]

'THE LAST ENEMY TO BE DESTROYED is death' (1 Corinthians 15:26). I have received many testimonies about death. In the next chapter, we shall look at how God spoke through the pain of bereavement to a number of people; here we look at the survivors. Our four stories could scarcely be more varied. In the first, Ian literally cheats death through a sovereign act of God; in the second, Randy discovers the power of God as his apparently dying baby recovers – but it then takes many years before God gets a hold on his life; in the third Dave wrestles with depression and suicidal thoughts after becoming a Christian; in the fourth a friend survives serious suicide attempts and emerges into a new life as a Christian.

A Glimpse of Eternity

Ian McCormack *lived a normal carefree life until his encounter with a box jellyfish in 1982. Since then, he has devoted himself to telling people of the reality of God's judgement and his offer of grace.[1]*

Ian McCormack's story is, by any standard, remarkable. Ian's testimony begins with his disillusionment at his confirmation service in New Zealand in the 1970s. At the age of fourteen, he expected to hear God speak to him. He embarrassed his father, his parish priest, and his mother, with his questions. He walked away, announcing that he would never come back to church. As he stamped off to the family car, his mother, uncharacteristically, yelled at him, 'Son, if I can teach you nothing else – remember one thing – however far you find yourself from God, if you cry to God from your heart, he will hear you and forgive you.'

For ten years, Ian lived a carefree life. He sought pleasure in sport, travelling, surfing, and especially in scuba diving. Visiting the island of Mauritius in 1982, he enjoyed some magnificent scuba diving, catching huge lobsters, avoiding sharks...

All went well until one night when his torch picked up an interesting looking box-shaped jellyfish. He squeezed it with his leather gloves. Unlike the others in his party, he wasn't fully protected, and in return for his inquisitiveness, he received four stings from the deadliest jellyfish known to man – known as 'the invisible one' to the locals. One sting can kill a man in ten minutes.

By the time a terrified teenager got him to the shore, he was already paralysed on one side. The boy panicked and left him. He crawled into the middle of a road at 11 p.m. without much prospect of a rescue. The poison made him sleepy. He heard a voice saying, 'Son, if you close your eyes you shall never awake again.' Moments later he crawled around a bend and found three taxi drivers. He heard the voice say, 'Son, are you willing to beg for your life?' Ian begged the taxi drivers to rescue him and to trust him to pay them later. Two laughed and walked away, the third agreed (with the promise of $50) to drive him to hospital. The third driver took him to a tourist hotel, decided that he would never pay his fare, and physically pushed him out of the taxi.

At the hotel he met a friend, Daniel, who couldn't believe that he'd been stung by 'the invisible' and wasn't yet dead. Three Chinese proprietors of the hotel wouldn't take him to hospital. He could feel the coldness of death creeping up his body; he knew enough veterinary science to know exactly what was happening to him.

Eventually, an ambulance arrived, because his Creole friend Daniel had phoned the hospital. On the way to the hospital his whole life flashed before him. He knew that he was going to die. Then he saw his mother, in a clear vision, praying for him in the ambulance… she began to share the same words with him that she had spoken after his confirmation. He didn't know which God to pray to, but decided that as his mother would pray to Jesus he'd better try that. He tried to remember the Lord's Prayer. In a jumbled fashion, it came back to him. 'Forgive us our sins.' Ian tried to list his sins, but settled for admitting his hypocrisy, particularly his desperation in turning to God at such a time. The next phrase that came to him was, 'Forgive those who have sinned against you.' He didn't feel there were many people that he needed to forgive.

Then he saw the face of the Indian taxi driver who had pushed him out of the car. 'Will you forgive him?' 'I wasn't planning to!' Then he saw the Chinese who had refused to take him to hospital. 'Will you forgive him?' Suddenly he realized that, to use a New Zealand expression, this was where 'the rubber meets the road'. Either he forgave these people, or he couldn't be forgiven. He prayed, 'If you can forgive me, I will forgive them'. The third phrase of the Lord's Prayer that he remembered was 'Thy will be done, on earth as it is in heaven'. He submitted to God's will, admitted that he'd been rebellious and wrong for twenty-six years, and promised to follow God for the rest of his life. He then remembered the whole prayer, and received a great sense of peace.

After arriving at the hospital, every emergency treatment was tried – without success. After about ten minutes, a doctor said kindly, but clearly, 'Son, I'm afraid we've done all we can for you'.

His eyes closed, he gave a great sigh of relief, and he found himself wide awake in a pitch black void. He had a huge sense of terror, he realized that he was 'out of his body', yet conscious. He said, 'Where am I?' Two voices spoke in the darkness. The first said, 'Shut up', and the second, 'You deserve to be here, shut up'. Then one of the voices said, 'You're in hell – shut up!' and Ian heard the voice that he had heard when lying on the road saying, 'If you hadn't prayed that deathbed prayer in the ambulance that's where you would have stayed'.

Then he saw a brilliant light, and he was lifted up into the presence of an incredibly brilliant, but distant light. Waves came from the brightest source and filled his body with warmth, comfort, peace, and joy. He was drawn closer to the source of the light which was as radiant as a mountain of diamonds. He wasn't sure whether the source was personal or impersonal.

Then the voice spoke again, 'Ian, if you return, you must see in a new light'.

He remembered words on a Christmas card that he had received, 'God is light; in him there is no darkness at all'. (He didn't know that this was a biblical text – 1 John 1:5.)

Ian felt completely unworthy, but wave after wave of light touched him, filling him with love and more love. Weeping, he cried out, 'I want to see you'. He felt a great healing radiance, and saw a man's feet, but where the face should have been there was a brilliant, dazzling light. (Afterwards Ian read Revelation 1:13–18 and recognized what he had seen as corresponding to John's vision.) He was able to see behind the form of Jesus, and was shown a vision of paradise, with green pastures, mountains, blue sky, trees, and a crystal clear stream (again, afterwards, Ian read Revelation 22 and 2 Peter 3:10–18 and recognized much of what he had seen). He remembered that he had travelled the world looking for such a place, and asked, 'Why wasn't I born here?' The voice replied, 'You've got to be born again, Ian, now that you've seen, do you want to step in or return?'

He wanted to say goodbye to the sick, tired world. No one would miss him. He had no debts. Then he remembered his mother. If he entered paradise, she would assume that her prayers had been unanswered, and that he had entered a lost eternity. He saw that Jesus was the door to paradise, leading on to green pastures (again, afterwards, he read John 10:7–9). He knew that he must speak to others to give them the same chance that he had been given, and he chose to go back.

The voice said, 'Tilt your head', and he woke up to see a terrified Indian doctor who was prodding his feet. He tilted his head the other way and saw the look of blank horror on the faces of the nurses and orderlies in the doorway of the room where he had been laid out – apparently dead for fifteen minutes.

For a moment he thought he had returned as a quadriplegic. He prayed, 'Lord, if you can't heal me...' Ian then felt an extraordinary warmth which lasted four hours, then he knew that he was completely healed. He walked out of the hospital the next day. None of the locals could face him. They thought he was a spirit who had returned, and they were terrified of him (a reaction not unlike those who prayed for Peter's release from prison!).

Ian, in his account, says quite humbly that he believes he died, but that others may prefer to interpret his experience in line with Paul's vision recorded in 2 Corinthians 12:2–4 where Paul writes with tantalizing brevity about an 'out of body' experience in paradise.

Perhaps the most amazing part of his testimony was the experience of his mother, who, exactly when this drama was happening, woke up hearing a voice, 'Your son is nearly dead – pray for him'. Ian McCormack is not the first person, nor the last, to owe his salvation, humanly, to a godly, praying mother!

A Life over Death Encounter

Randy Vickers *has had a successful business career. He was brought to faith in 1975. Five years later, after training, he was ordained in the Anglican church and combined his business career together with non-stipendiary ministry. In 1991 with his wife Dorothy, he founded the Northumbrian Centre of Prayer for Christian Healing. Randy has recently published a book:* The Anointing to Heal.

In 1960 our eldest son Michael was born. At the time I was nominally a Christian, having been baptized and confirmed into the Anglican church. It was not until fifteen years later that I experienced a personal encounter with God and knew that I was born again.

Dorothy and I had married in 1959 in the Catholic church. She was raised Catholic, her family was Catholic and her grandmother who had been the mainstay in her life had a real and deep commitment. Before the wedding could be permitted the parish priest had to lead me through the required number of lessons covering those things that would be expected of a non-professing spouse; this included promising that any children of the marriage would be baptized in the Catholic tradition.

Within hours of the birth it was diagnosed that Michael had a respiratory problem which could only be dealt with at a different hospital some twenty miles away. He was whisked away from Dorothy who was left deeply troubled and anxious at losing her baby from her side.

Visiting Michael was a deeply disturbing experience. This tiny little baby connected to lots of tubes, lying naked in what seemed to be a huge incubator. I could only stand and look at him in despair, trying desperately to think of something hopeful to say to Dorothy at visiting time. We had been married for less than a year and were facing this huge tragedy confined to meeting in a large open ward for only one hour each day. There was no opportunity to really be together, to hold each other or share our grief.

I cannot remember whether two or three days went by before Michael's doctor came in to talk with me on my visit. He had seen from the records that Michael was listed as Catholic and advised that the hospital priest should be called to baptize him, as there was little hope of his maintaining his tiny hold on life. Within what seemed minutes the priest had arrived and a Catholic nurse agreed to act as temporary godmother. Her name was Nurse Riley, I will never forget her name, and even now, forty-five years later, my eyes have filled with tears and my heart with sadness as I recall that bleak time.

From the baptism I drove to the appointed hour for visiting at the maternity ward. I could not find the words to tell Dorothy what we had just done. I could not tell her that they held out so little hope for her baby that we had gone ahead and baptized him without her knowing.

In my mind having him baptized was confirmation of our understanding that he would die. But I did not know my Bible, and even if I had I could never, at that stage in my life, have believed the truth of the word and anticipated what might happen when we brought him to meet with Jesus in baptism. Something happened when Michael was baptized. He immediately started to respond. Life returned to that tiny spirit. The respiratory problem disappeared. Within two days, as I recall, he was strong enough to be returned to his mother's side. From then on he thrived. I did not understand it, but I just knew within myself that something miraculous had happened.

Michael and his wife now have three children of their own and he is an Anglican priest. But that is another story of another encounter with God.

An Encounter with God:
Father, Son and Holy Spirit

In 1975 I was not searching for any inner, deeper or greater meaning to life. I was far too busy building a business for any of that kind of nonsense. In 1973 I had moved from a famous major company where I was general sales manager to a much smaller organization. The objective of the move was to create a new enterprise, in which I was to become a partner, if it proved successful.

Dorothy and I had been married for fifteen years and we had three boys aged fourteen, twelve and nine. Dorothy was teaching full-time. I seemed to be working twenty-four hours a day and was frequently away overseas in Asia or Europe to meet suppliers and seek out customers or else I was touring round the UK to see every potential buyer in the kingdom. Although at this stage the company was virtually a one-man band, I was already seeing success with customers such as Boots and Woolworths and many other well-known names in retailing and wholesaling.

At weekends I was usually involved with my sons and very early on most Sunday mornings, before the family woke up, I would be found playing golf. Also in 1973, Dorothy and I had moved to an old Edwardian house which needed a lot of renovation: complete redecoration, installing central heating, stripping out beams with woodworm, replacing ceilings, replastering walls. Because of our limited income much of this had to be DIY.

During the previous year we had been invited by our next-door neighbours to join a fortnightly discussion group which had been one of a number formed during Lent by the Council of Churches in the town. When Dorothy told me of the invitation, which she had accepted for herself, I had no good reason to refuse, especially as we did very little together as a couple.

It was a pleasant group of people, from a number of denominations and was led by an elderly Catholic couple who only lived two doors up from our house. Their modus operandi was to choose a book with some kind of Christian ethic which members would read, and we would take turns to lead the ensuing discussion. They insisted on referring to us as Christians even though Dorothy insisted that she was not. Dorothy had renounced her Catholic beliefs many years earlier but had been searching for the truth in the intervening years. I had been baptized as a baby and confirmed into the Anglican church as a youth but had long since ceased to have any connection with the church apart from at Christmas and Easter. So for us it was largely a pleasant academic exercise rather than a religious gathering.

For the previous Christmas, our leader's sister had given him a book, *When the Spirit Comes*, written by Colin Urquhart – the vicar of a church only ten miles away from our town. He decided that we should use it as the basis for our future discussions. The person responsible for the presentation at the next meeting totally disliked and disapproved of the book. He had not one positive thing to say in its favour. To calm the heated conversations which the presentation aroused, our leader suggested that we should all go to visit the church and see for ourselves. The only mutually acceptable date was found to be some weeks ahead.

Dorothy is a night owl and she borrowed the book that Friday evening and sat up until 4 a.m. reading. Then at such an ungodly hour she came to bed, woke me up and asked that we go to the church on that weekend rather than wait. Desperate for sleep I concurred.

Our friend Patsy came with us on that first visit to St Hugh's. It was a cold winter's evening but the church was packed and warm. I had never seen a church so full on a Sunday evening, since The Forsyte Saga had emptied them. I saw clergy with collars on and nuns in habits as well as ordinary folk filling the pews. The worship had already started when we squeezed in, but they were not singing hymns that I knew. The band and the singers leading the worship seemed to be on some sort of stage at the front. Many people had their arms in the air as they sang. I had to admit that it was extremely pleasant and had a lovely feeling. The singing must have lasted an hour itself. Some of it I learned later was singing in tongues. I had never heard of such things but our friend Patsy, who is an artist, described it perfectly as sounding like crystal snowflakes gently falling. Colin Urquhart spoke for some time. I still don't know what it was about but I know it was good. Everybody seemed very friendly.

As we drove home Dorothy and Patsy asked what I had thought about it and whether we could go back on the following Sunday evening. I agreed that we could. With regard to the meeting itself, I still felt a warm glow but boiled it down to the fact that Colin Urquhart must be a good motivational speaker. I was a successful sales manager who was able to motivate salesmen and stir them up at conferences and therefore decided that Colin must be of the same mould.

Colin was not there the next Sunday evening but the warmth and the pervading sense of love still filled the church. At sometime that Sunday night whether during the singing or the praying or the sermon I never could recollect, I met with God. My mind was filled with a picture of our town in which I was a member of the Chamber of Commerce. I saw my three sons being beaten in the Market Square; beaten, not by hooligans but by prominent traders, who were friends and colleagues. They beat them and then dragged them up to Windmill Hill, a grassed hill that rises from the top of the main thoroughfare. Then they put my boys on to crosses and hoisted them up high. I pleaded for them to take me and let my children go. I could do nothing to stop it. I heard God saying that I should forgive these people. I cried that I might if they did it to me but not to my babies. God said, 'I forgave you when you did it to my son'. In that time of seeing these pictures and hearing this voice in my mind's eye I just knew that God is real, that Jesus is real, that the Holy Spirit is real and that Satan is real. That Satan is not just a symbol of evil or enmity but that he is a real entity. How long it took, I don't know. It could not have been long because neither Dorothy nor Patsy noticed anything. That night I met with God and came into a personal relationship with Jesus.

From that time on my life changed.

*   *   *

David Ridge *works in IT; he is a long-standing member and lay leader in the congregation of Holy Trinity Leicester with responsibility for a number of cell groups. He has travelled on mission trips to Africa and South America a number of times, with me and others. He writes about his conversion and his later release from suicidal thoughts.*

I was brought up in a stable and loving family home but for some reason, from time to time, I was quite unhappy as a child. I don't actually remember a lot about my childhood but I recall on one occasion planning to poison my parents and on another standing in my bedroom with a knife to my heart wondering about killing myself. I was a boy scout and in those days part of the uniform was a sheath knife with a blade of about four inches. Quite why I considered killing myself I don't know, or even how serious I was or why I didn't. I don't recall if there were other times like this.

When I was eighteen I became a Christian and it was quite a radical change for me. My upbringing had been very strict so when I went to university I decided I would drink as much alcohol as I wanted, whenever I wanted, and have as much sex as possible. Indeed I chose a university quite some distance from home specifically so that my parents didn't visit me too often and so restrict my behaviour.

However, before I got too far with my plans I met some Christians. I thought I was a Christian as I had been taken to church every week as I grew up, and though I found the moral framework too tight for my liking I had never consciously decided not to be a Christian. I was never taught that one's behaviour and belief should be compatible! The Christians I met intrigued me because they took their faith seriously and yet seemed to be happy.

One day one of them came round the student rooms doing a survey about Christian beliefs. I answered 'Yes' when asked if I were a Christian but a subsequent question had me stumped. 'Why did Jesus die?' I had no idea, and felt I really ought to know. So when the guy invited me to look at this question through some Bible study I agreed. We had only had two sessions when I realized that Jesus died in my place, paying the death penalty for my sins. I knew that I wasn't a Christian but that I needed to be one. I was very aware of my sin because I knew that all that I was seeking to do, having thrown off the restrictions of my parents' boundaries, was wrong.

I changed overnight. The night I was saved I read the whole book of Romans under the bedclothes by torchlight. (I shared a room.) I was fascinated by Paul's explanation of sin and righteousness.

I grew rapidly as a Christian, not least because I endured

some strong persecution but also because I had a lot of discipling. The negative side though was that the Christian environment in which I found myself coupled with my aversion to anything that would lead me back into sin caused me to become a very legalistic Christian. After a few years I became convicted that all the rules I had built for myself were actually preventing me from being much of a witness as I never met any people who were not Christians, so I began to change.

It was very painful, although one of my friends who was captain of the rugby club became a Christian. This became quite well known as he was seen by other people who were not Christians as definitely not the sort to be religious! Nevertheless there was some emotional turmoil as I wrestled with false guilt. Looking back on my childhood and especially my teenage years I had been through times of stress and depression despite there being no obvious traumas.

These feelings of anxiety returned. When my finals came I only got through with the help of medication and God! After graduating I got married and a few years later three events coincided. Our second child was born, we moved house, and the company I worked for announced out of the blue that it was on the verge of collapse. A long period of stress and anxiety started. I became depressed and was prescribed the anti-depressant Seroxat.

It was during that time that I started to think about death. I'd think that I wanted to be dead and have thoughts in my head such as 'Why don't you kill yourself?' I remember on one occasion hearing what I can only describe as an external voice telling me to kill myself. I'd drive along the motorway and think that if I undid my seatbelt and just steered into a pillar holding up a bridge over the motorway than I'd end it all.

Eventually my depression lessened and I tried to come off the anti-depressant, but I had severe withdrawal symptoms. During all this time I had had leadership responsibilities in my local church which went through a big split; many people left, so my responsibilities increased. Because of this, I decided to go to a Christian conference about counselling and there I felt something changed. I felt God say that I could now come off the tablets and slowly and painfully I did. It was not an instant miracle, far from it, but I had hope restored and I stopped taking Seroxat.

From time to time as the years went by I'd get depressed but to a much lesser extent. I was once prescribed the tablets again when it got pretty bad but I remember sitting in the car looking at the packet of pills knowing that if I started I would be heading to a bad place. So I decided to try it without the tablets and never took them.

Although I never got as badly depressed again as that time, the thoughts of death returned, both the wanting to be dead and the frequent thoughts that seemed to come into my mind, saying, 'Why don't you kill yourself?' Again I'd think about the best way of doing this. When I heard of Christians being killed for their faith in other countries, I would wish it was me so that I could find a legitimate way to be dead. The thoughts seemed to be something that was happening to me over which I had no control.

At various times I'd had people pray for me for my feelings of depression and once or twice there had been quite a strong reaction – I would move suddenly and involuntarily. But the thoughts of death kept coming. After a while this got me down in itself – it was like having a friend who kept telling me to kill myself every time I met them! So I booked a long time of prayer with two of the staff at our church.

I think I was a bit embarrassed – it was not what I thought I should be thinking. I told my story and together we tried to listen to God. The two people praying with me were very experienced, and yet I felt that none of us quite knew what to pray for or even how to pray. Often on these occasions it is our experience that God will reveal something that acts as a sort of key to unlock the situation – I've known that happen a number of times. But on this occasion that did not happen and there was no physical reaction to prayer like I had had before. Consequently, I was a little disappointed when we finished. Some time later, however, it occurred to me that the thoughts of death had gone. The whole experience had been about as un-dramatic as it could have been and yet it had worked.

A few years on, I have to say that I have had these thoughts very rarely; if they do return, it is with much less intensity. I have learned to treat them as a warning sign that something is not right, and to take control of them rather than letting them take control of me (see 2 Corinthians 10:4–5).

Surviving Suicide

James Charles *has come through a lengthy period of psychosis and psychiatric admission and has experienced remarkable healing. He now helps other people who are troubled in this way; he is married with two children.*

For now we see in a mirror dimly, but then face to face. Now I know in part, but then I shall fully know even as I am fully known. (1 Corinthians 13:12)

In the midst of crisis, our fears can overwhelm us. None of us can predict the future. In times of extreme emotional pain we can be deceived by hopelessness, feeling that 'it will always be this way', because the feelings are so strong at that time that any alternative cannot be possible. This is so far from the truth it is dangerous.

As a twenty-one-year-old undergraduate in my final year at university, I was so overwhelmed by fears that they became my reality. I lost all hope for the future and past. I believed the overwhelming feelings I had at that time were the only reality I had known or could ever know. When in that darkness, it is near impossible to believe there is even such a thing as light.

I tried two serious suicide attempts. The first involved overdosing on painkillers and waking up in a ditch. The second consisted of lying down on a railway track waiting for a train to come – and it did! I remember being in the darkness of a tunnel at Birmingham New Street station. I saw the yellow light of a train approaching. I lay between the rails on the track. I felt a thud as it connected with my back; then my head was pushed into the ground. The train ran over my body and my hand which was on the tracks. I lost track of time. I was in a lot of pain. I lifted my hand and saw my little finger hanging off it.

Some paramedics arrived and I was admitted to intensive care. I could not walk. My hearing had gone. My sight was blurred. My back pain was agony. In the hospital, I found that it was difficult to be still, nor could I move. Gradually I regained full physical health with a missing finger as the only remaining permanent damage. I see this as God's mercy, similar to Jacob's hip (Genesis 32:31), to remind me that it did really happen and how I could have been disabled or killed. My finger is all that God took from me for my drastic actions.

These suicide attempts were rational responses to the apparent unbearable. I wanted out. But the unbearable is not real and is not true; life will not always be that way.

If I had succeeded those thirteen years ago, I would not have experienced the many blessings and experiences of life – all the people I've met and the friends I've made, having faith in Christ, realizing that there is a God who loves me, enjoying fruitful jobs and ministry, the gift of beautiful children, marriage and home life. And yet beyond all that, God promises us so much more when we meet face to face.

Even at our most insightful, at best we can only see a reflection of God and wonder at the future. We just don't have the faculty to fully appreciate the richness of a future with God. We cannot know our future on earth, let alone comprehend a future with God. It would be the greatest regret to have missed out on the above things by succeeding in suicide thirteen years ago.

I am now involved in suicide awareness training. In our country we have some 'enlightened thinkers' who consider it a dignified privilege and ultimate freedom of choice to commit suicide. This is such a tragic mistake. By permitting the ultimate hopelessness to be valid, we deny the possibility of hope and God's love to show itself.

Faith is trusting through the darkness. If we never know darkness then our faith can only be theory; waiting to be put to the test.

Conclusion

These four walked, in very different ways, near the valley of the shadow of death; they experienced God's grace and protection in remarkable ways. Neither the survival of the encounter with the box jellyfish nor with the oncoming train have any rational explanation – God intervened!

Now we look at a number of testimonies of people for whom the outcome was more painful. God is sovereign; sometimes he provides remarkable protection and/or healing, sometimes he comforts us in our difficulties. The early church discovered this when they lost James, one of the three closest to Jesus, to the sword of King Herod while immediately afterwards an angel was sent to rescue Peter.

Note
1 A video of Ian McCormack giving his testimony, *A Glimpse of Eternity*, is obtainable from St Andrew's Church, Chorleywood WD3 5AE.

6

God in the Valley of the Shadow

[Walter Moberly*/Judi Morton*/Clare Prichard*/
Christopher Turner*]

ON 13 JUNE 1969, MY MOTHER DIED at the relatively
young age of fifty-seven. On the night of her funeral,
I read the words 'I tell you the truth, you will weep and
mourn while the world rejoices. You will grieve, but your
grief will be turned into joy' (John 16:20). It didn't seem
very likely. As an only child, I was trying to support my
father who was liable to depression. Then I read the next
verse which was about a woman in the pain of childbirth.
The words spoke to me; Scripture had seldom spoken so
powerfully. Shortly before she had died, I had, uncharacteristically, taken my new girlfriend to visit my mother in
hospital. My mother had been very pleased and full of
hope for my future. The words of Scripture seemed like a
confirmation that this relationship would prosper – and
indeed it did!

The immediate months ahead were very difficult. In
the summer, I started ordination training at a very liberal
theological college. My faith was severely challenged and
not helped by an alcoholic relative who wrote 'I can't
think why you are being ordained. Your prayers didn't do
your mother much good!' My father slid into deep

depression; his doctor, a good family friend, and I watched helplessly. In November, he took his own life.

In that terrible darkness, I was much helped by many friends. The Bishop of Winchester, a kindly, godly man, redirected me to train at St John's College, Nottingham where I met Michael Green who was to have a big influence on my life – not least when I served as his curate in St Aldates, Oxford. In the turmoil, I clung onto faith particularly remembering the words of Peter: 'Lord, to whom [else] shall we go? You [alone] have the words of eternal life' (John 6:68).

Here are some more testimonies of how God helped people through their personal times of bereavement and spiritual darkness.

* * *

Walter Moberly *is an ordained Anglican. Since 1985 he has taught biblical interpretation and theology at Durham University. Since 1986, he has suffered from ME. He tells of his first wife's unexpected death and its aftermath.*

I would like to say something about the worst night of my life: the night my son was born.

My wife Meredith had had an increasingly uncomfortable pregnancy. During a particularly bad weekend, she was taken into hospital and, since she was already at thirty-five weeks, the doctors decided to deliver by caesarean. On the Monday afternoon, while some pre-op tests were done, I had a coffee in the hospital canteen. I had a slight sense of foreboding, and I thought back over our almost ten years of marriage.

It had not been an easy marriage for much of the time. Meredith had suffered years of bad depression, and I had somehow acquired ME (aka chronic fatigue syndrome). At one stage we had raised the question whether we might split up. Yet we had come to a place where our marriage felt the stronger for all that we had been through; we loved each other deeply and unreservedly, with joy and delight in each other. There was everything to look forward to.

After being with Meredith late afternoon and phoning family and friends to tell them what was happening, I then sat in a waiting room in the evening while Meredith was taken to the operating theatre. Quite quickly a lovely sleeping baby, John-Paul, was brought out, and I spent time with him stroking his head as he lay in a special cot. But Meredith was not brought back. My instincts told me that the longer she was kept in theatre, the worse the prognosis was likely to be. I waited another two hours, looking sometimes at a card that our friends David and Sally had brought round with its message: 'The steadfast love of the Lord never ceases, his mercies never come to an end' (Lamentations 3:22, ESV).

At about 10.30 p.m. the consultant and another doctor came to see me. They came directly to the point. When they had looked inside Meredith they had found her gut full of cancer, to an extent that was beyond operating. Although they did not say so in as many words, they made it clear that she was going to die very soon.

I sat numbly in a waiting room, until I was able to go and see Meredith in post-op. She was drifting in and out of consciousness, and I sat with her holding her hand. I finally returned home to an empty house at 2 a.m. I lay on the bed in anguish, and prayed. This was the night when I was wrestling like Jacob, as before God I confronted the knowledge that I was going to lose the one who meant everything to me. Over the next few hours, two passages and images from Scripture were at the front of my mind: God telling Abraham to sacrifice his beloved son Isaac; and Jesus praying in Gethsemane, 'If it be possible, let this cup pass from me; yet not my will, but yours, be done'.

There were no flashing lights or voices from the sky. But by morning, two things had happened. I had come to accept that Meredith was to die, but that she and I were in the Lord's hands. And I had been cured of any lingering desire (a temptation for a theologian) to 'justify the ways of God to man' – there was no good reason for Meredith to die; yet lack of understanding could still go hand in hand with trust.

Meredith lived for another 114 days. We tried aggressive chemotherapy in the hope not of cure but of postponement. It made no difference (except that Meredith's hair fell out, though she characteristically wore colourful headscarves with style). Many friends prayed for her recovery. I never joined in, for I knew from my night as wrestling Jacob that she would die. Yet Meredith and I each had a strong awareness of being in the Lord's hands. The practical love and support from friends was wonderful, so that John-Paul was well looked after. At the funeral, our good friend David Day articulated the pain and anguish so honestly that the strong Christian hope of resurrection with which he finished his address was entered into not as mere words but as living truth.

After Meredith died, for the first year, the anguish felt like physical pain within. My body shut down, and I lost two stone. I slowed down, and would not drive faster than 50 mph on an open motorway. I spent countless hours at Meredith's grave. One time, after going to the cinema to see *Rob Roy* with a friend who was helping with John-Paul, and feeling deeply moved by the ending where, after life had been risked and death had been confronted, Rob Roy was able to return safely to his wife and children, I quickly excused myself, went to Meredith's grave, lay on it, and just sobbed and cried, and sobbed and cried. Yet beneath the anguish remained the sure knowledge that I was in the Lord's hands.

I was particularly dreading the first anniversary of Meredith's death, as a time when the anguish would be even worse. I set the alarm for 5 a.m. so that I would be awake at the time she died (though I woke then anyway). From that first moment of waking and throughout the day (though not at all on the following day) I had the strongest continual awareness of God's presence that I have ever had, so that the day was marked by tears of thanks and trust.

It took me months within that first year before my heart could deeply connect with John-Paul, simply because I was so numbed by the loss of Meredith. Yet while I was having a quiet day at my favourite retreat in Alnmouth the Lord nudged me and made clear that I must attend more to my precious son (who within the womb had been kept safe from the cancer beyond). So I learned to take true delight in John-Paul; although seeing Meredith's eyes in John-Paul's eyes would constantly reduce me to tears.

In the second year I remained numb, but less so. In the third year my feelings started to return to normal; though it wasn't until four years had passed that I was able, with help from Karen (who with her husband Andrew are godparents and guardians to John-Paul, and supported me unceasingly with practical help and hospitality) to sort through and give away Meredith's clothes. Throughout this time I was given care for John-Paul, space to grieve, generous and supportive friendship; I am lastingly grateful to Carolyn and Graham, Andrew and Karen, Sally and David, Martyn and Joyce, Patricia, and many, many others.

Four and a quarter years after Meredith died I met Jenny, and we had a whirlwind romance and got married within two months and a day of first speaking to each other. I am grateful I did not meet Jenny sooner. Despite the speed with which some people recover from bereavement, especially in novels and films, I was not capable of forming any new relationship, in which I would not simply project Meredith onto someone else, for a full four years (I did in fact try at an early stage within the bereavement, but thankfully the woman had the wisdom to say no).

I learned that anguish can keep company with a trusting confidence of being in God's hands; that mind and emotions can play endless tricks, and need firm moral and spiritual disciplines; and that there are no short cuts through the valley of the shadow of death. The steadfast love of the Lord indeed endures for ever; and I have learned, I hope, not to understand this glibly.

* * *

Judi Morton *writes: 'As someone who "never did God" I look back at the time before December 1999 with amazement. As I sit here in a dog collar I seem a million miles away from the person I used to be in the financial industry. I am no longer interested in the fancy job title, perks and good salary but am only interested in helping others find a relationship with God and helping them realize that their is more to life than meets the eye. I have been changed by God and for that I am extremely grateful.'*

The day was 14 December 1999. That day I had been so low that I actually lay on the floor sobbing my heart out and wishing I was dead. That was in the morning. Between the hours of midday and 2.30 p.m. my life was completely changed.

Some fourteen months earlier I left a company called Northern Rock where I had worked my way up the ladder from cashier to area manager covering the whole of Merseyside and the Wirral and where I had been employed for fifteen years. Getting promoted was nearly impossible because nobody ever left!

I left to join a smaller and more local building society where I would be doing the same job but would be more involved and nearer the board and therefore my ambitions might be achieved faster. As soon as I took the post, I had misgivings. Nothing was in place for me. The goalposts were constantly moved and what I had been told at interview was not what was going to happen. Infighting at the most senior levels was prevalent and to cut a long and unhappy story short, I walked out of the job.

On the outside, I looked as if I was totally in control; but at home, when alone, I felt awful. John, my husband, and Tricia, my best friend, who had supported me and helped to give me the self-belief that I had needed, had all their work for the last fourteen months undone.

Tricia, who worked at a senior level in the Royal Bank of Scotland, had said that I had a good case for constructive dismissal because the promises made at interview had not materialized. She was fighting breast cancer and had been doing very well, but now seemed to be getting a series of infections. I had visited her on 20 November – the only time that we talked about death – and she asked me to speak at her funeral. Her father would speak about the first part of her life, then I was to take over. I couldn't possibly refuse even though every part of me was screaming, 'Me? Talk?' I never saw Tricia again; she went into a rapid decline and died six days later. My last words to her made her laugh.

Then I went to see the vicar. I asked him if it was all right to make people laugh! He prayed for me and I went home feeling better and after thanking him, I told him that he wouldn't see me again as 'I don't do church'. I knew, instinctively, when Tricia died. I had prayed that she would be allowed to die with dignity and peacefully; I knew the moment she died.

The day before her funeral, I went with her boyfriend Robin to Holy Communion. We went because I had hardly ever been into a church, let alone spoken in one. I was very nervous about speaking and wanted to check it out. We went with Tricia's sister and her husband Lindsay, who, unbeknown to me, were Christians.

During the service, I felt bathed in a spotlight and was really embarrassed. No one noticed. I just put it down as another strange experience. Then the funeral day came; about two hundred people were present. I spoke and I don't think I have ever stopped speaking since! After the funeral, and at the end of the party, Lindsay put a bag containing three books in my hands. He said, 'I've got to give you these, Jude. I don't know why, but you must have them.'

When I saw what they were, the three books were flung into a far corner and there they stayed until midday on 14 December. Those three books helped to change my life! They were *The God Who Changes Lives*; *Questions of Life* and the *Why Jesus?* booklet. I read them in that order; they dealt with every ounce of my cynicism and I said the prayer at the end of the *Why Jesus?* booklet. Time seemed to stand still. All the anger and hatred that I had felt against my former employers, and about Tricia's death, left me. For the first time in my life, I felt whole. Whatever had been previously missing; was now present. I was changed! I was God's – and he was mine.

The following morning at 9 a.m., I had the most amazing experience of his love. It was all around me, within me, above me, below me, it was all encompassing. I knew then that he lived and that Tricia lived in eternal life because his promises are true. They are not make-believe as the world would have us believe.

Before her death, Tricia had been visited by the vicar who had done a quick Alpha course for her. It was only when I started an Alpha course the following January, that I found out that she had given her sister instructions to get me on an Alpha course. She wanted to make sure that I would find what she had found in the last period of her life. I have and she, in death, has given me infinitely more than I ever gave her in life. I thank Tricia for that – even if it has turned my life upside down.

Within a couple of months of becoming a Christian, I knew that I was being called to be ordained. When my friends joked about it, I became snappy; inwardly, I knew that I was serious about this strange new step.

In July 2000, I was sitting in my study, thanking God that within months of regaining employment, I had been promoted to area manager for the bank – which had to be God's work, as I vowed I would never go back to banking. Then a bizarre set of events had changed all that. I was thanking God for my promotion, when I heard myself say, 'But this isn't what I want to do. I want to do your work.' I don't know why I said it, but I did. God took me at my word. I heard, audibly, 'Read Isaiah 58 and Ezekiel 3.' I didn't know that it was possible to hear God speak. I jumped a mile and cried 'What!' God repeated himself. I couldn't believe it.

Having been a Christian only seven months, I had to

chuckle to myself: 'I've made this up; there won't be fifty-eight chapters in Isaiah and who is Ezekiel?' When I found both books, I was blown away! Each chapter started 'Go tell my people!'

Despite this, I said that I wouldn't go and speak to my vicar. If God wanted this to happen, the vicar would have to come to me. And, of course, he did!

Six years later, after doing the Bishop's foundation course for ministry and reader training, I still couldn't avoid the call to ordination. My ordination course at St John's College, Nottingham finished this year, and I was ordained on 30 September 2006. To say that God had moved quickly in my life is somewhat of an understatement. But I do feel certain that I have found what I was born to do.

*   *   *

Clare Prichard *is a widow with three sons, Charles, Andrew and David, who are twenty-four, twenty-two and twenty years old respectively. Her husband died of cancer in 2002. She lives in Hampshire, between Basingstoke and Reading, and is involved with speaking and discipleship counselling for Freedom in Christ Ministries (UK). She also spends a large proportion of her time helping people with nutrition.*

All my life I have had a strong belief in God and I have been a regular churchgoer. One of my childhood dreams was to be a missionary. My parents brought me up to believe as a matter of course that God was real and could answer prayer and work miracles. I remember at the age of seven being at a mainly Jewish school and being stunned that one girl didn't believe that Jesus was her Messiah. I spent ages trying to convince her. However, although I knew lots about Jesus, I didn't actually know him.

After leaving school I went to Durham University to read classics and had many friends, some of whom were training for ordination. I went out with one of them for a while and had this idealistic idea of becoming a vicar's wife with dogs and children flying all over the place.

In 1979 I married Peter, who was an engineer in ICI rather than a vicar. We did, however, go on to have two dogs and three sons. I was thrilled that he had a strong belief in God as I had always felt that this was an incredibly important point to look for in a husband.

We lived in Yorkshire when we were first married and had many very committed Christian friends. I could never work out what it was that they had that I lacked. My life became increasingly filled with children and my interior decorating business. I had eight people working in our home and there were pattern books and lengths of material strewn all over the place.

After nine years we moved down to Hampshire and I started attending the two local churches. I became more and more conscious of the need to have a deeper spiritual life. One day, I met an American on a train up to London and we exchanged addresses. When he gave his wife my address she was decidedly unamused and tore it up. However, three weeks later I bumped into the American and his wife at the local church. They came for tea that day and as a result of our conversation I started thinking really seriously about Christianity. Other friends too encouraged me in my Christian walk and I even joined a Bible study group.

About nine months later I was attending another church and saw the pastor praying for a girl. I felt a terrific urge to go forward for prayer myself. I decided to postpone this until the next time. I didn't tell anyone about my decision and at the next service, during the worship, the pastor suddenly stopped the service and said that he believed that there was someone there who wanted to have a real relationship with Jesus Christ. The pastor never did this on any of the following Sunday morning services and it could only have been that he heard directly from God that caused him to say what he did. I shot off to the front of the church. He prayed for me, and at the time I didn't feel anything and even the headache that I had didn't go away, but in the next few days I soon found that I had an incredible new hunger for anything to do with Christianity. I had a committed Christian working for me and would ask her endless questions. When she went home at night she used to apologize to God and tell him that she could not face talking about him any more that day. I devoured book after book and went on the first ladies' Alpha course outside London at Malshanger, where I came to understand more about the fullness of the Spirit and how he can help us in our Christian life.

One of the most amazing things I found was that when I went to the local church, the traditional Anglican service suddenly came alive and words that I had been saying for years took on a completely new meaning. Going to church meetings and conferences was something of which I could not have enough in the early days. I felt increasingly that time was precious and that I should be contributing in some way and not simply filling my life with meetings for my own self-indulgence. I remember being told of a dream about a football stadium. In the dream, God said that you had the choice of either being a spectator in the stands or a player on the pitch where the action is.

In 1994/5, I did a biblical studies course at Waverley

Abbey. One of the many things which really struck me was the way that the Jewish people and then the early Christians were called by God to be concerned with the fatherless, the widows and the poor. One evening, after a talk given about the prodigal son, I felt that God was telling me to work with the poor. I then listened to a number of tapes by Jackie Pullinger, who has done tremendous work amongst the destitute in Hong Kong. She talked about the need for every single Christian to be working with the poor and that it wasn't an option but a necessity. Following various other events I found myself volunteering to work in Reading for a furniture redistribution charity for the poor called Christian Community Action (CCA). I worked for CCA one or two days a week for three years. Initially, my work involved interviewing the people who came in to find out what they actually need as opposed to what they wanted in the way of furniture and also to find out whether there was any other help required, either with regard to physical needs or emotional problems. After a while, I moved on to the CCA charity shop and organized a book room at the back of the shop with twenty-two bookcases. I reckoned I had the biggest library outside Reading library. It was a wonderful environment to talk to people about Jesus.

After about three years of working for CCA, I went to a conference in Reading, where I came across an American called Neil Anderson, who was the founder of Freedom in Christ Ministries in the States. This is a ministry which helps people resolve their spiritual and personal issues. As a result of this conference I ended up leaving CCA and being involved in Freedom in Christ. I am still with Freedom in Christ to this day and have helped with administering and taking discipleship counselling appointments and being part of the teaching team speaking at churches around the country.

In April 2002, my husband started having bad stomach pains which became more and more severe. Six weeks after first visiting his doctor we were told that he was terminally ill with cancer of the pancreas and liver. My initial response was one of shock, but then I felt that this must be God's opportunity for him to come to faith in Jesus, and that God would heal him.

Peter had been a bit shocked by my conversion but as the years had gone by had come more and more to terms with it. My Christian faith, however, had been an area that we never talked about, which was a great source of sadness to me. As part of his preparation to go into a hospice, the head came to see us. She happened to be a friend from our church, and asked Peter about his spiritual life. He told her that he had peace with God and that his maker would look after him. This was the most tremendous comfort for me and especially when he died two days later, four and a half weeks after the diagnosis. The boys and I were absolutely devastated at his death but amazingly, even on the first day I had a real sense that God still had a exciting future plan for my life. I read my way through the Psalms in the early days and again and again God reminded me that He was with me. He has truly been my shield, my fortress and my strength. I never felt angry with him for the outcome. I had learnt so much about health and how our diets, the toxic world we live in, and so on can have a huge impact on our bodies. I felt, therefore, that in many ways we only had ourselves to blame.

His death, however, has given me a tremendous desire to help others with health issues and to pass on all that I know. My hope is that out of Peter's death other people's health will be improved or lives extended. My walk with God has been a real adventure. My only regret is that I spent thirty-seven years of my life not knowing Jesus, but he has truly made up for the years that the locusts have eaten.

*   *   *

Christopher Turner *was formerly Headmaster of Dean Close and Stowe. He is now, as a non-stipendiary minister, a member of the ministry team of Hook Norton, Great Rollright, Swerford and Wigginton, a benefice of about 3,000 in Oxfordshire. He is married to Lucia who is herself a lay pastoral assistant in the team of ten. Along with the rector, another curate and a licensed lay minister, Christopher shares responsibility for leading services of worship, preaching, teaching and occasional offices. It is now the policy of the benefice to have considerable lay involvement in all areas of Church life and worship.*

Three children were born to Christopher and Lucia: Rosalie in 1962, Matthew in 1964 and Kate in 1967. They have three grandchildren.

The first time I heard Graham Kendrick's song, *The Servant King*, was at our daughter Rosalie's wedding: she married Roly on 19 December 1987, in Stowe Church. That made the song very special to us, not least because it reflected her own humble commitment, pilgrim style, to our saviour. What follows in the story I'm about to tell made the song even more precious.

In 1988 I had to decide whether to retire in 1989 or 1990; whichever I chose would have the governors' blessing. The prospect of service shared with Lucia in 'fresh woods and pastures new', free from the socially restricted sphere I had enjoyed since childhood (though with growing restlessness), was tugging me away from an idyllically beautiful place and endlessly exciting responsibility.

There came a day when some act of adolescent stupidity (the sort that happens routinely in schools), and the pressure (against my natural inclination) to take it seriously just tipped the balance, and I said to Lucia, rather out of the blue, 'I've had enough; I must go in 1989'. The plan forming in our minds, and very much a major topic of prayer, was to find some way of bridging the gap between the familiar superficially 'comfortable Britain' (Bishop David Sheppard's phrase) and the complex urban world where most of our fellow citizens lived and struggled.

The academic year 1988–89 was our last in full harness. Plans for the future were left to simmer, for our focus had to be the school. School wasn't our only preoccupation. Our children needed support and I know I failed them in that respect in their most formative years. Matthew and Kate were beginning to find their way in the world; Roly and Rosalie, at St John's College, Nottingham, were preparing for his ordination in July and their move to Deal.

We had a day's holiday in February. We drove up to Rosalie's home, and spent a few hours with her, walking on the rim of Dovedale and lunching together in The Bluebell. I remember being concerned that her glands were not quite clear of the old fever. That evening we joined in the College Communion with them both. What a precious day! We next saw Roly and Rosalie on our final Speech Day, a day of strongly mixed emotions. Rosalie was keenly interested in our bridge-building plans, and in the weeks that followed would chat about them with friends and report back their reactions to us on the telephone.

June was to be the last full month of term, our last, and the month of Rosalie and Roly's move. My approaching retirement was interwoven with Rosalie's last weeks in Nottingham. An important date for us was to be a special party for saying thank you to prep school heads, on 20 June. One of our preachers in the school chapel that year was our area bishop, by then a very good friend and an invaluable source of wisdom and support. He was very keen to know our plans for 'retirement'.

I told him of our hope to find some way of bridging the great social chasm in our society. 'You are, of course, talking about priesthood,' he said. I replied that I had assumed that such bridge-building was inevitably a lay calling. 'Quite the opposite,' he said gently, and he then explained. His words stayed with me and in our prayers; I knew God would make the whole picture plain in his own time.

It was Fathers' Day on 18 June. Rosalie sent me a card, in spite of their impending move. We sent them a card to their Deal address, welcoming them to their new home. On the 19th, Lucia drove all the way to Kent and back, to attend the funeral of an old friend. I was unwontedly agitated – but she came home safely.

Tuesday was dominated by the evening party. We had both wanted to ring Rosalie, but both missed the opportunity. Guests arrived for the party, and it got off to a good start. Towards the end of the meal, which was going very happily, I was called out to answer the telephone. It was Roly. Rosalie had been killed that afternoon in a road accident...

God carried us through the days and weeks which followed. Close friends were very angry with him; we ourselves were trustingly bewildered. Why should he have Rosalie back so soon? Well, perhaps he knew she was exceptionally ready. But she still had so much to give. God convinced us that she would go on giving a great deal. We were always conscious of God's presence; most wonderfully, he gave Lucia the courage and inspiration to speak to the school in Chapel a few days after the event (she was already propping me up), and soon after that he helped me through my final sermon (on the prodigal son), on the very day of Roly's ordination.

But the love and support of family, friends, colleagues, governors, parents and pupils went beyond words. There was a deep, deep void, but we floated along on love. Plans for the future had to be shelved until emotions were less raw and unpredictable. Rosalie we knew was safe, and she has played a very, very big part in our lives and ministry ever since.

In August and October 1989, we went ahead with our planned holidays in India and the USA. Matthew and Kate made us feel they understood – but had we given too little thought to their needs? They certainly gave us a huge welcome home on our return each time. In November, Lucia and I had our intensive immersion in Liverpool's problems. It was admirably organized and we met heroic men and women working cheerfully at the coalface. ('Have you had some successes?' 'That's not what we're here for; we're here to be with them.') The dedicated imagination we saw was exhilarating; and we felt sure we were moving in the direction God had planned.

At first, we had explored a call to Liverpool; but that door seemed to close, and we were put in touch with a friend in Birmingham. Guy Hordern became for us the gatekeeper into the complex world of Birmingham's deprivation and to the superb, many-faceted response to it from Christians and secular activists. We visited Guy on 1 March, and had a few days of an experience matching, and moving us on from, Liverpool. Prayer underlay and illuminated it all.

Our attention was unexpectedly drawn to the plight of the

outer estates which were as deprived as the inner city, but without the support given to designated 'UPAs' (Urban Priority Areas), and therefore were worse-off. On advice from the Archdeacon, to whom we related as to another man sent from God, we spent two weeks in early May, as a follow up to the March reconnaissance, in Chelmsley Wood and King's Norton.

Again, we met with warm, practical encouragement. Our hosts made sure none of our time was wasted. Lasting friendships were made. Of the two areas, we felt that Chelmsley Wood had made a little more progress towards a renewal than King's Norton. For me, the pivotal moment was Sunday 9 May. We attended a confirmation in the Hawkesley Anglican-Methodist church/school in King's Norton. Mike Whinney, an old friend, was the presiding bishop. (Strangely, the last time we had met him had been with Rosalie and Kate, at a washed-out royal garden party three years earlier.) The music? *The Servant King*. Those being confirmed were of all ages, all lived locally. I was utterly overwhelmed with the sense that we'd come home.

After that, we prayed step by step, consulting the archdeacon again, and assurance grew in us that we were to buy a second home in a quiet, but vulnerable area adjoining the roughish Pool Farm. We were helped in the purchase of the house by the proceeds of insurance on some treasures stolen when our home was burgled three months earlier. Another coincidence? So began our ten-year association with Hawkesley and Pool Farm. It was a part-time link, because the intention of bridge-building stayed with us. Our principal task was as voluntary classroom assistants, primarily with children with special needs, and it was such a joy to be working together locally.

Meanwhile, lay ministry in our home village revealed a compelling need for a resident minister. The villagers seemed aggrieved that 'the church' had removed their vicar and attached them to Hook Norton – what has West Oxon to do with Cherwell or Yorkists with Lancastrians?!

One lady in particular, who has become a very good friend, unintentionally made clear the need for a resident ordained pastor. I was already in touch with the bishops of the diocese; there was no doubting their hopes. The selection conference in the late summer of 1991 endorsed their hopes and the spiritual impact of the conference gave me another experience of God's personal intervention. Thus it was that God led us into a wonderful, but tiring, ten years of being linked to two very different worlds. We learned so much more than we gave. My ministry training began in 1991 and continued after ordination in 1992. By that time, our new rector had arrived in Hook Norton and we have worked and prayed with him happily ever since. But, until December 1999, we would spend forty-eight hours a week during term-time in Hawkesley School. Lucia added adult education to that and I was honorary treasurer of a nursery – we found some great friends and we had a lot of fun.

'So let us learn how to serve,
And in our lives enthrone him...'[1]

Conclusion

Bereavement, as it always does, proved a great challenge to all my contributors. This is a spiritual and emotional challenge that we are unlikely to avoid. It is part of the journey 'through the vale of misery' which the psalmist describes in Psalm 84. In the psalm, which is mainly an idyllic spiritual journey to Jerusalem, we are encouraged 'to use it for a well' (Prayer Book wording). I have seen men and women digging under dry rivers in Tanzania searching for water in times of drought. In bereavement, there is much need for spiritual water; our belief is that if we search, God will show us how to find it. Often, we will have to let other people do the digging, but the water is always there.

Note

1 *The Servant King* by Graham Kendrick © 1983 Thankyou Music. Adm. by worshiptogether.com songs excl. UK & Europe, adm. by Kingswaysongs.com, tym@ kingsway.co.uk. The full words and sheet music for this song can be obtained from www.kingswaysongs.com

7

Healing Signs

[St Augustine*/Nigel Mumford*/Wendy Haslam*/Alice
Mason*/Peter Hancock*/Howard Barnes*]

H EALING IS ONE OF THE SIGNS of God's kingdom presence. Experiencing healing can transform the direction of someone's life; it can also revitalize the faith and
ministry of a church. These testimonies bear witness to
the effect of God's healing grace in some very different situations.

In the first three centuries, the early church witnessed
many healings. By the time of **St Augustine of Hippo**
(354–430), the miraculous seems to have largely died out.
Augustine wrote that Christians are not to look for the
continuation of the healing gift. He assumed that such
gifts were no longer needed or available. He changed his
views, and towards the end of his life wrote:[1]

> Once I realized how many miracles were occurring in my
> own day... and also how wrong it would be to allow the
> memory of these marvels to perish from among our peo-
> ple. It is only two years ago that the keeping of records
> was begun here in Hippo, and already, we have nearly
> seventy attested miracles.

He gives details of many of these. One of the most dramatic was of a devout Christian called Innocatius, a leading citizen of Carthage. He was suffering from dangerous

and painful ulcers. He had several unsuccessful operations. An eminent surgeon declared that there was no hope without another operation. But the church had other ideas.

Augustine tells how they devoted themselves to prayer. Innocatius was deeply affected and prostrated himself as if someone had forcibly thrust him down. The surgeon arrived, accompanied by their dreadful instruments. When the dressings were removed in preparation for the operation, the surgeon could find nothing wrong! There was much joy and gladness. Augustine adds 'the scene may be more easily imagined than described!'

Such things continue in the twenty-first century!

*   *   *

Nigel Mumford *was serving in the Royal Marines Commandos; the unexpected healing of his sister led him to become a Christian. Praying for others led to a call to ordination in the Episcopal church of America and he is now director of The Oratory of Christ the Healer at Christ the King Spiritual Life Center in the Albany Diocese.*

I am a former Royal Marine Drill instructor. I spent nearly eight years as a green beret commando. I spent a year on active duty; I was shot at three times and blown up five times. I almost drowned in Malta in a scuba diving accident. I was seventy-five feet under water on my first dive with no training! Not a good idea! My mask filled with water, I panicked, and bolted to the surface. The weight belt was too heavy and I was not wearing an ABLJ life jacket. Having reached the surface, I could not stay afloat and after a while I began breathing in water. I lost consciousness. Unbeknown to me, I was rescued by another diver, resuscitated and rushed to hospital where I spent three days recovering.

I consider myself very lucky to be alive. Upon reflection I think that God had a plan for my life that is in total juxtaposition to being a drill instructor, he spared my life because '"I know the plans I have for you" declares the Lord, "Plans to prosper you and not to harm you, plans to give you hope and a future"' (Jeremiah 29:11). He knew the plans he had for me, but I certainly had no idea what was going on!

I have missed death at least nine times: if I was a cat, I would be very nervous now! I am a cradle Anglican; but my faith was really tested as I witnessed the sickness of my sister, Julie Sheldon. I kept asking, 'Where are you God? What is it with this dreadful illness that has afflicted my sister [a ballet dancer]?' I have to say that I was a nominal Christian before my sister's dramatic healing. I had become quite hardened because of witnessing man's inhumanity to man in combat; humans can be so cruel to each other. After moving to the USA I started to receive frightening phone calls from my parents reporting on Julie's rapidly progressing undiagnosed symptoms.

For the first six months of a very painful three-year illness Julie was misdiagnosed as having 'a hysterical condition'. 'Go home to your kids,' she was told over and over again. (Her full story is told in *Dancer off Her Feet*, Hodder and Stoughton, London, 1991 & 2003.) Her leg had drawn up in a most crooked way; she could not walk, let alone dance! Manipulation under a general anaesthetic was carried out. The leg straightened by force and contained in a plaster cast as if the leg was broken. Shortly after the anaesthetic had worn off the leg went into spasm, Julie screamed in agony and passed out and then her leg cracked the plaster cast!

The cast was immediately removed. Shortly afterwards, Julie was diagnosed with dystonia – a neurological disease that sends the wrong messages to the muscles. Over the next three years, the disease progressed to generalized dystonia. Her time was spent going in and out of the intensive care unit to the point where, up to ten times a day, all her muscles would contract and then expand to the point where the prognosis was death by breaking her own neck because of the violent body contractions.

The last time I saw Julie in this condition, she weighed about 75 lbs. She was being fed through the nose and looked like she was ready to die. I am ashamed to say that I considered killing my own sister because of the pain she was in. I thought of using a simple manoeuvre taught in the Marines. I thank God that I did not, she would be dead and I would be a murderer. I am embarrassed to write of this but I want you to know the severity of the situation. I left her hospital room in tears having said my goodbyes...

I wondered around the streets of London feeling quite hopeless and lost. I found myself in a WHSmith bookshop and was drawn to the military section where I found a book with a photo of a Commando on the front. It was a book about the Royal Marines. I flipped through the book and found a photo of myself that I did not know had been taken. The photo was of me on the death slide at the commando training school in Lympstone, Devon. It was not until later that I realized Julie was on her own death slide, a couple of streets away. The salesman at the register was not in a good mood, so I asked him to open the book at that page. He looked astonished and announced to everyone in a very loud voice, 'Look here, there is a photo of this man when he was in the Marines...' Many people thronged the register to look.

I was embarrassed but taken out of my major funk in seconds. Upon reflection it was as if God himself was telling me something. A divine appointment with a photo in a book that I did not know even existed! I travelled back to the USA that evening a very sad young man. The very next day however, Canon Jim Glennon came to visit Julie. Canon Jim had a wonderful gift of healing and his books (*How can I Find Healing* and *Your Healing is Within You*, both Bridge Publishing, New Jersey) [PC30]teach powerfully about the healing ministry. Canon Jim believed for Julie's healing and prayed for her with the laying on of hands. That afternoon Julie sat up and the next day she even got out of bed and hopped to the window. Julie had been healed by prayer. Even Professor Marsden, a top neurologist quoted in *The Times*, said, 'Julie has made a miraculous recovery'. Julie is now completely healed of this disease; a disease that normally does not go into remission.

Not long after this happened I had a life-changing experience. I owned two picture framing businesses in Connecticut, USA, employing eight workers. One day a woman walked into my shop looking dreadful. I asked her if she was OK. She told me that she had a very bad headache. After finishing the sale I walked around the front of the counter. What happened next was totally out of character at that time. I looked her right in the eyes and watched my hands, totally involuntarily, rise very slowly and then rest upon her head. My mind was racing: what are you doing Mumford? I asked myself. It was not at all appropriate. She could have screamed assault. I thank God that she didn't. I have to say I have never done anything like that in my life before. I just saw my hands lifting as if my wrist had been gently held and guided to her head. What happened next was totally life-changing.

I felt like I was in a daze and that what happened was all rather surreal. I thank God for what I have now learnt. Please understand, I am not boasting, I am just telling you what happened. Acts 13:15 says: 'If you have a message of encouragement for the people please speak'; Psalm 105:1–2 says: 'Give thanks to the Lord, call upon his name; make known among the nations what he has done. Tell of... his wonderful acts'; and 2 Timothy 1:8 proclaims: 'Do not be ashamed to testify about our Lord'. I write this to give all glory to God because he is the healer.

As I touched the woman's head she looked me right in the eyes and said, 'What did you do? The pain has gone!' That hit me like a ton of bricks, that one sentence; those eight words just had such an effect upon my life that I am not sure that I can even put it into words. The realization was that I did not do anything, but surely God did! She was healed immediately of a wicked headache. The colour returned to her face and now she had a big radiant smile.

Since that moment in 1990 I have sold my business, run a home for healing, moved from Connecticut to upper New York state and now I am ordained as an Anglican/Episcopal priest and run the healing ministry centre at Christ the King, Spiritual Life Centre for the Episcopal diocese of Albany. I thought I wanted to be a policeman and then a marine for life. But God had other plans! My vocation now is to pray for the sick; I have written about this in *Hand to Hand: From Combat to Healing* (Church Publishing, New York, 2005). My new book, *The Resurrection of the Forgotten Touch* will be out in the autumn of 2007.

I for one can surely testify to the hope that is within me because of the hope that is within Christ as he calls us to preach the kingdom and heal the sick (Matthew 10:7–8). This encounter with God in witnessing the curing of my sister has brought me to a totally new relationship with God to a point where I have taught about the healing ministry at three of the top seminaries in the USA and at Wycliffe College in Oxford. I have also spoken on the ministry of Christ's healing in front of four hundred American doctors at a conference at Johns Hopkins Baltimore, the largest hospital in the world. I have to say that I am surprised and humbled and still very much in awe of what a wonderful God we have.

* * *

Wendy Haslam *is married with three children. She has been a reader in the Church of England for many years. She is a trained counsellor and has recently set up the Still Waters centre in Wedmore in Somerset.*

In the early 1970s I lived in Malawi, Africa with my husband and two small children. Life was good. The sun shone upon us and we enjoyed the freedom of it all with friends. We had a good life.

That was, until I began to have pain from my neck. I had an old neck injury, received when I flew off a motor scooter in my teenage years. I had, perhaps through playing tennis, aggravated the injury and set up a pattern of serious pain; as well as the pain, I had headaches which made me feel sick.

I lived with this pain until one day after I had been playing tennis, my neck seized up. Having seen the local doctor, I was told that I needed urgent treatment and was thus flown down to what was then Rhodesia. Tests followed and surgery was recommended. However, I was told that there was a 50 per cent chance of being left paralysed. Not a promising outcome.

I was fitted with a ridged collar and declining the option of surgery, flew back to Malawi to think it over. Meanwhile, unknown to me, a group of people were praying for my injured neck. At this stage in my life I was not a Christian.

One afternoon, as I lay on a bed on the veranda of our house, someone called Sue, who was part of the praying group, came to see me. She told me that as a group of Christians they were praying for healing for my neck. She offered to pray for me right then. This was the first time that I had received such an offer. I declined. She very graciously complied with my answer and I was left to continue to sweat it out in the pain and heat of the day.

It got hotter and hotter as the days went on and the pain increased. Because of the pain, I could no longer pick up my small son. That really hurt me inwardly. It motivated me to think that I needed to take further action. One morning I made a decision. I would give this Christian healing a try and, if it did not work, I would fly down to Rhodesia for the operation.

I set off from Zomba with my two children and drove to the mission station in Blantyre, where Sue and her husband then lived. The mission station was not far from the airport so I was all ready for the next step if it did not work.

It was another hot day. I recall that we spent the morning talking as the children played. Sue's husband Ken arrived home for lunch and afterwards the children were put to rest. Then, the three of us knelt down on the cool concrete floor, around a small low table, and prayed. On the face of it nothing dramatic happened. I remember both Sue and Ken asking for the healing of my neck and for wholeness for me. I wondered 'What did they mean by wholeness?'

Afterwards, we sat and talked. We then had a little walk

around the mission station. As I walked, I began to feel a sort of 'lifting' within. I felt lighter. I knew I was to return home to Zomba. As I travelled home, with the bright sun in my eyes, I realized that my headache was lifting. Remarkable! When I arrived home, it began to dawn on me that something amazing was happening. I no longer felt sick. I felt different.

That evening we went to a house group. As I walked in, people remarked that I looked different. What had happened to me they asked. It looked and felt as if I was walking on air. I could not stop smiling. I told them about the day and how Sue and Ken had prayed for me. I don't really remember anything else about that evening except that the rest of the group were very excited. Yet I still could not take it on board. Bear in mind that I was not yet a Christian.

The next morning I woke up and felt really good. No headache, no sickness and still the feeling of walking on air. With help I removed the fixed collar. I then picked up my basket and went to the market. For some months I had needed someone to carry the basket for me. Not so today. As I purchased my goods so people talked to me and asked what had happened. Word soon got around. Something big had happened. The next few days seemed like a dream.

I could not stop smiling. It dawned upon me that I had been healed. I knew nothing about healing at all. Malawi is a small country. News travelled fast. Soon I, along with others, was part of an explosion of faith; in the midst of it all, I became a Christian. We had no books as such to tell us what to do.

I found myself embraced in love and surrounded by a new family – a Christian family. I discovered that I had a desperate need to read the Bible. The words seemed to jump out at me. I suddenly began to understand the Scriptures. I began to pray with others. We prayed for further healings. People were healed. People were converted – the greatest healing of all.

I saw people healed in front of my eyes. God was at work in a way that few had ever seen. That was the start of my Christian journey so I thought it was how God did things! I assumed that it was normal!

Just as an aside – at that time Francis McNutt was in another part of Africa. Years later I talked to him in Wells Cathedral. He discovered that I had lived in Malawi. He asked me if I knew of the girl who had been healed in Malawi in the 70s. I replied, 'Yes, it was me!' He told me that the healing had had a ripple effect – much healing resulted in the Congo when that news reached them there and increased people's expectation.

To continue my story – I was then baptized and confirmed and my life as a Christian was sealed. Soon, all too soon, we left Malawi and returned to England.

So my Christian journey continued. I became a lay reader and was very involved in Christian counselling. Then in 2000 I realized that I was very unwell. That was the start of the battle with an infected kidney, which remained undiagnosed for several years. My health deteriorated over the next few years and I was in constant pain.

So it was that in 2002, I found myself in a hospital bed, with an epidural to address the severe pain. I was very ill indeed, low in spirit and wondering if my life really was ending. As I lay there, in a side room I heard an audible voice saying 'still waters'. I decided that I must have been hallucinating. A little time later, a man entered the room and came up to me. He introduced himself as a doctor. Saying that he did not usually do this sort of thing he told me that God had told him to tell the person in my room that 'Whatever I had been told to do I must do it'. We talked a little and he told me that he was to return to his home in Cape Town the next day but that he and others would pray for me. And so he departed and I was left wondering what these two words meant.

I shared this experience with a few people and we prayed. I began to slowly recover. I thought that God was asking me to form a counselling and training organization in the South West that was to be called Still Waters. It was a very long haul back to health but as I did so, I began to work on the formation of Still Waters. A wonderful American girl called Patricia who lived locally was inspired to create the logo. Together we spent hours working out the details of what would be offered and she designed a leaflet. And so Still Waters was born. Working with a small team, we have continued to journey on as we reach out to the needs of those around us. It has and continues to be an awe-inspiring journey with him. Just as, so long ago the Lord changed my life, so we now, through the power of the Holy Spirit, offer that healing and wholeness to others. I am most richly blessed.

*   *   *

Alice Mason *was born in 1964 in Norfolk and as a child lived for a few years in Australia. She received a BA Hons for Fine Art from Bath Academy of Art in 1986. After that she lived in London, the Cote d'Azur, and Los Angeles for five years where she was a mural artist. She speaks French and adores singing. Her husband Nigel is a photographer and they have two children, Eleanor Rose and Remy Laszlo. The name Laszlo comes from Lazarus, meaning 'God Has Helped'. She says: 'It is my life's mission to live as much as*

*possible as Jesus taught us. To try to be non-judgemental,
love other people and to be humble. To appreciate everything
as the miracle it truly is, to live in love rather than fear. Fear
is a feeling of separation from God.'*

My first realization of my encounter with God happened, as
it very often does, in difficult circumstances. I had been
through long-term troubles with the travel business that my
husband and I ran from our home. Finally, the business went
under, after huge amounts of stress, and I was coping with
scores of irate customers yelling at me down the phone on a
daily basis. We had a little holiday home in France which we
knew we had to sell as quickly as possible. This saddened me
as a second home in France had been a lifelong dream. On
top of this, I discovered I was pregnant.

We already had a beautiful daughter, but I had suffered
from post-natal depression after her birth and I had long
since been fearful of that happening to me again. Another
pregnancy was not something I had consciously desired. It
hit me very hard. Things became rather too much and those
first few weeks of pregnancy were extremely difficult. I began
to suffer terrible panic attacks. A combination of hormones
and my business situation meant that I was practically
unable to eat anything. I was suffering severe migraines and
all-day 'morning' sickness coupled with depression and anxiety. I was wandering about in a daze; instead of blooming, I
found that I was losing weight and my heart rate was racing
constantly.

One day, during one of those early days of pregnancy, I
was picking up my daughter from her choir practice at the
beautiful church in Winchelsea, where she goes to school.
Ellie is a lovely friendly little girl, and she always wants to

know what's going on. At the time, there was a mission taking place over several days in the churches of Winchelsea and Winchelsea Beach. One of the people involved was the missioner, John Woolmer. I remember Ellie wanting to ask John what a missioner was, and I accompanied her while she asked him questions and he answered her questions. I began to realize that this was someone that I needed to speak to.

We all walked outside and I spoke to John about my panic attacks and pregnancy. He seemed so very intuitive and I strongly felt that he knew where I was coming from. After leaving the church that afternoon, I felt the faintest glimmer of hope, for the first time in weeks, months. I bought one of his books, *Healing and Deliverance*, and he gave me a copy of *Angels*. John told me about the healing ministry and I went home and took the book upstairs to my room to read.

The next few days I met with the ministry and poured out my heart to the wonderful people working alongside John and to John himself. We prayed together, I talked about my past, parts of which I had felt so burdened by for the longest time. It was such a relief to talk to a priest about these things, which had so troubled and pained me for so many years. The pain and fear were slowly beginning to depart. I felt lighter.

The prayers that were said, the kindness I felt from these wonderful Christian people – I had never known such kindness. I began to really feel the healing power of Jesus' love and to understand, at last, what Jesus was about. At last, I received inner knowledge and the beginnings of a deep peace. I somehow felt that Jesus was holding my hand and guiding me, if only I would allow him to do so. Once in a while, over the next few days, I actually felt a glimmer of happiness. I had almost forgotten how happiness felt. I began to eat a little more.

Prior to meeting John and the ministry, I had visited different spiritual healers on three different occasions while I
was pregnant, but for whatever reason, they didn't get to the
heart of my pain, and it was not alleviated. Somehow I felt
that through John and the ministry I was finally getting in
touch with God. I had prayed for so long and finally my
prayers were being answered, something was unfolding.
Through the collective spirit of all these good people and
their love and healing prayers I was finally allowing myself to
be healed and to encounter God.

I had to allow God to take over. I was being over-vigilant
and over-controlling and resisting and fearing change,
thereby resulting in panic attacks. It had not been my plan to
be pregnant in difficult circumstances, but I realized it was
God's plan for me, in order to be healed. I was learning that
the next baby could have been sent to heal me. I now know
this to be true! I had always known in my heart that a second
baby was my only true way to healing. After all, I am a great
mother, and love babies and children.

In this modern, stress-addicted society, we get so caught
up in the material world of instant gratification, instant
remedies, instant 'solutions', always having to be in charge,
goals, game plans. If something unexpected comes our way,
we feel we have to 'get back to normal', to get back to our
game plan. We are afraid of the unknown, because we have
lost contact with God. To let God show us the way seems to
be the hardest thing to do sometimes. But in fact, it is the
easiest thing to do, once we relinquish control and allow God
to take over. Sometimes God has other plans for us.

After John Woolmer and the mission had gone away from
Winchelsea, I was starting to feel better. I knew the path I had
to take, and I began reading and praying, looking for and

finding God everywhere. Once you look for God, he is everywhere.

I logged onto a website, by tapping 'depression in pregnancy' into Google and found myself on an American website called Babycenter.com. Americans are far more proactive about getting help and articulating their emotions in so many ways. I put up a message on the message board and checked in the next day, and there was a message from a woman called Cathy from North Carolina.

This was an answer from God, pure and simple. It was my intention to find some form of spiritual help in the form of a friend in similar circumstances, and God gave me Cathy. Cathy was pregnant too, and living in the Bible belt, was definitely a Christian, but someone like me, who can 'think outside the box'. Her mind was highly intelligent, enquiring, loving, sensitive, and she had suffered bouts of depression over several years, similar to myself. The bond was instantaneous. She was like my American female soulmate, we were so unbelievably similar. We even looked alike in ways, both very tall, with long red hair. Our life stories too had incredible parallels. It was uncanny. Intellectually, emotionally spiritually, we were so alike. We emailed each other every day for the rest of our pregnancies, and beyond, after our babies were born. We helped each other, because we were not alone. We still email and phone each other. We have become best friends although we have never met. I love Cathy with all my heart. Our babies are now almost two years old, and Cathy is now expecting her third child.

If you look for signs of God, they are everywhere. But you have to intend to see those signs. I now cannot understand anybody who doesn't believe in God. To me it is an absolute impossibility not to, but God cannot be understood by the mind, because thinking is too limiting. Through 'not' thinking we encounter God; through the state of no-mind because God is beyond time and space. He cannot be conceived of through the limited ways we use our brains. We have to switch our brains off to really feel and know God. Thinking too much removes us from knowing God, in my opinion.

When all is said and done, the most powerful physical and spiritual encounter with God, to my mind, is to give birth to a child. The sheer unbounded miracle of childbirth and creating a new life is utterly mind-blowing and the most amazing embodiment of God's power.

I am so grateful to have gone through that time of difficulty because I now see everything as miraculous. How I didn't see it before is beyond me! I must have been asleep my whole life!

Once I decided to let God guide me, things truly fell into place. We easily sold our French house and my husband Nigel was awarded a full grant as a research student, one of only twelve in the visual arts in this country, to do a PhD in his specialist subjects: photography, architecture and philosophy, combined. Because of this, we had some money for the next few years, and Nigel was able to be at home with me and our beautiful baby boy Remy when he was born. At first, we just sat in the garden in the warm spring weather and gazed at him with love and awe.

Two years later, I have been baptized, along with my two children, and Ellie and I confirmed. Ellie serves at the church twice a month and I attend as often as possible. I try to do everything with love in my heart and I have changed in so many ways. I feel God's presence in every aspect of my life.

*   *   *

Peter Hancock *was vicar of Broughton Astley, south of Leicester, for eleven years. Later, he was the diocesan healing advisor for Bath and Wells. We travelled together in Zambia during a memorable SOMA trip in 1992.*

Hebrews 11:10 speaks of Abraham living in a tent, yet looking for a city which has foundations, and whose architect and builder is God. I put those words on my desk in the rectory at Broughton Astley in the early seventies, and this short article is a witness to their truth in the lives of ordinary people.

In the early summer of 1973, our family moved to Broughton Astley, where we were to begin a new period of our ministry together. St Mary's Church had an Anglo-Catholic tradition which suited my background, and the PCC were glad to have a youngish priest with a small family – the two previous rectors had stayed on until reaching retirement age. I had been away from parish work for eight years, serving as diocesan youth officer in the Diocese of Portsmouth, so we were glad to return to a congregation which we would call our own.

I suppose that the congregation was as one would expect for what was known as a Catholic parish, with Sunday Mass being the centre of our worship. Outside, the influence on the church upon the life of the parish seemed to centre on a garden party and a bazaar. It is the function of the local congregation to present an exciting, possible alternative life centred around Jesus; but this concept seemed to be miles away from the normal life of the church. People thought of those who worshipped at St Mary's as simply another organization similar to the British Legion or the Women's Institute!

Things changed in Lent 1975. Ever since my ordination, I

had read as many books as possible on how to run a parish. As Lent began, I picked up a small book called *When the Spirit Comes* which was written by Colin Urquhart, who at that time was completely unknown to me. The book spoke about the moving of the Holy Spirit in the lives of members of Colin's congregation at St Hugh's, Luton. I remember putting the book aside after a few pages, because I thought that the author's claims were so arrogant!

Broughton Astley was growing as more and more houses were built. A lovely young couple, Philip and Heather Carver, moved into the village and began to attend the church. Titus Kuyebi, a gracious Nigerian, was also part of our small congregation; soon the four of us began to meet to pray for our village. One day, Philip asked me if I intended to go into Leicester to hear a priest called Trevor Dearing speaking about renewal.

I listened as Trevor told us of a great awakening to the Spirit in his own church in Hainault, near Chelmsford. As he spoke, I began to realize what John Wesley meant when he said his spirit had become strangely warmed when he first realized the truth of the gospel. That is how I felt, as I listened to stories of changed lives, of miracles, and of the coming of the Spirit upon the church in Hainault. Then one of the people present asked Trevor, 'Can such a moving come upon villages as well as town churches?'

I said to myself, 'Yes, and He will come upon our church too.'

And He did! On Good Friday, I stood in my church after everyone had gone home, and told the Lord that I was fed up with being mediocre. He said to me 'They that wait upon the Lord shall renew their strength; they shall mount up with wings as eagles; they shall run, and not be weary; and they shall walk, and not faint' (Isaiah 40:31, KJV). I had no idea where those words were; but I knew they were for us. I knew that the Father would do for us the same wonderful things which I had read about in Colin's book and which I had heard Trevor speak about.

Now everything seemed different. I had known Jesus as my personal Saviour and Lord since childhood; but no one had ever taught me about the person and work of the Spirit. But very soon, I and members of our congregation were to discover the wonders of God's gracious moving amongst us.

People came to know Jesus, others who had been members of the congregation for many years were changed, others were healed of various illnesses, and more and more people came to join us to find out for themselves that what the Bible says is true. We began to act as if Scripture was true – and it became so to us as we believed.

We invited a well-known healing evangelist to visit us once a month, and our church was packed to the door. People came from all over the country; they wanted to know Jesus and to be healed. I put up a notice on our board saying 'Expect a miracle every day', and this was what we did!

We never knew what would happen in our church worship, or who would be the next person to come to know Jesus. We began to long to know more of the Word of God, and to expect that the Father would hear and answer our prayers. As more people came to new life in the Spirit, we saw his gifts manifested amongst us just as the early church had experienced. We saw the life of the church beginning to be effective on the lives of others living in Broughton Astley. It was no longer our lives, but the life of Jesus that was seen. It was no longer a garden party or the annual church bazaar that gave us the opportunity to influence other people; it was the leading of the Spirit.

Years later, as I write this, I know that this awakening for us then is the desire and longing of the Father's heart for all his people now. People do not see their lives changed by ideas, concepts, or by reading strange invented ideas of Christianity; but by a living encounter with Jesus. It is the Holy Spirit who brings about such meetings.

I believe that God spells words differently from us; he spells faith R-I-S-K. We risked a lot in 1975; we moved in faith and expectancy; but only in answer to the prompting of the Spirit. The renewal and revival were never of our making. They were from God, a God whose word and will is that we know him and that we should spend ourselves speaking of his amazing love and mercy. He longs for his people to know his loving touches and his desire that we should be forever his, and his alone.

*   *   *

Peter travelled several times to Zambia with SOMA teams. On the first occasion we travelled together to Chipili in the Luapula Province.

In the early nineties I was on a mission on behalf of SOMA to Zambia with John Woolmer, and we were posted to Chipili in the north of the Diocese of Northern Zambia. Here we found a very large church, and an enormous congregation on all of the four days during which we were ministering.

On one occasion at a healing service, I was praying for the sick together with the local archdeacon, Tobias Kaoma, when a young woman was brought up for prayer. She was quite small and slight, but four strong men were finding difficulty in controlling her. One of the men had a small baby whom he said belonged to the girl. When we asked about her, we were told that she was possessed by evil spirits because she had contacted a local witch doctor after the birth of each one of her four children, all of whom had died as a result.

I recall asking our interpreter to tell her that the child whom she now had would live, because she would be freed by the power of blood and name of Jesus from every evil spirit which bound her. I spoke to the evil spirits in the name of Jesus, and commanded each of them to leave the girl in the power of his blood. Then she accepted Jesus as her lord and saviour, and we prayed for the anointing of the Holy Spirit to be with her. On the following day two of the ushers who had been with her at the previous healing service brought her up to the front. She looked and was completely different. She was calm and confident, and now knew that Jesus, not the evil spirits, would direct her life.

We saw many other amazing things happen. Many people needed deliverance, many people were healed and there was great joy in the Cathedral church. John also got involved in raising money to help finance piped water for the area at the top of the hill where there was a school and where the church leaders lived.

* * *

Howard Barnes *worked as a schoolteacher in Cornwall. For many years, he felt that God was calling him to work overseas. Eventually, after witnessing the remarkable healing of a pupil, opportunities to serve the Lord overseas opened up. At the age of fifty-seven, he founded HfCNM (Harvest for Christ Networking Ministries) which is dedicated to seeing the body of Christ throughout the world healed and restored*

so that she can fulfil her destiny in God by finding her true
identity as the beloved bride of Christ.

I have a passion for his Church. Despite the wonderful things
that God, the Spirit, is doing in the world today, the church
of Jesus Christ, his body, still remains a very broken body. It
doesn't matter where you are, what country you're in, the
same situation exists: disunity, jealousy, bitterness, corrup-
tion, sleepiness, personal agendas, isolationism and inde-
pendence. The body is broken and dysfunctional because it is
dismembered. How can the church see herself as the bride as
long as she remains a divided body? How can she get dressed
and ready for His coming? How can you dress a dismembered body? The bride doesn't even know who she is... and
the Bridegroom is coming! She is so disjointed. Jesus prayed,
'Father... I pray that they may be one as we are one' (John
17:20).

It was during a 'Body and the Bride' conference in
Bushenyi in June 2006 that we were able to see a demon-
stration of the greatest miracle possible, a miracle of reconciliation and unity between ministers of his church.

Before that we ran the three-month mission throughout
Kenya, Uganda, Rwanda and Malawi, in May, June and July
of 2006. I had been shown so much by the Lord, about his
church and his bride as I spent time in his presence. It had
thrilled my heart but I had never had an opportunity to teach
it and to see the fruit of that ministry.

As we gathered church pastors and leaders together and
taught them during the 'Body and the Bride' conferences
throughout those three months, in four different countries,
we saw the fruit; we witnessed the Holy Spirit changing
incorrect 'strongholds of the mind' regarding the church and

the kingdom and witnessed the Lord Jesus bringing about a deep unity amongst the leadership. We saw ministers accepting their responsibility and earnestly desiring to 'dwell together in unity' in order to 'command the blessing' (Psalm 133, KJV). We saw the Holy Spirit move on their hearts in repentance and forgiveness and reconciliation. Old wounds were healed and his love was 'shed abroad'. This was by far the most precious and thrilling miracle that we saw, even though we had witnessed many mighty miracles of healing and deliverance. Such reconciliation tangibly changed the spiritual atmosphere of the cities and towns where we ministered and resulted in the birth of an effective citywide church.

The example that illustrates this best is the story that unfolded in Bushenyi, Uganda, in June 2006. It is recorded in an email that I sent to a dear friend and prophetic leader, John Mulinde of Uganda. I have included here an extract from it.

Dear John,

The invitation to work on behalf of The Way of the Cross Committee in Malawi, the host movement for the National Prophetic Prayer Rally, provided me an opportunity to travel throughout the land for three weeks before the Rally, and to speak to hundreds of pastors and church leaders.

What unity and love and repentance we saw amongst the brethren as the Holy Spirit took the teaching and ministered it to their hearts. In Bushenyi, Uganda, for example, 600 believers including 250 pastors from that city came together for four days. There was such a healing. After the conference we marched around the territory declaring on the posters that they themselves had written... 'We are the Pastors of

Bushenyi. We are one. There is now only one Church of Bushenyi'.

Our march took us around the city where we drove stakes, pipes with Scriptures implanted in them, into the ground at the four corners of the city, claiming it for Jesus Christ. There was indeed an open heaven, a shift in the spiritual atmosphere over the city, afterwards.

How do I know? Well, as I was walking back from the last place where we hammered in the stakes, back for the celebration time at the conference centre, we passed the witch doctor's house. 'Oh,' they said. 'He is a very powerful man in this area. He controls it!'

'Rubbish! How dare you say that!' was my reply, and the 'Lion of Judah' roared once again in my spirit! You have just committed high treason. He has no authority but you have just betrayed the King of Kings and given his authority over to another!'

I realized afresh that that was a prophetic statement and that the force and clarity of that word had come from God himself. I trembled! I went into the garden of his house and the witch doctor came around the corner towards me. He was stripped to the waste and bore the scar marks of his trade upon his chest and arms; deep welts crisscrossed his torso. I went up to him and said 'Hello! I'm Pastor Barnes from the UK. Come here brother. May I give you a hug?' And do you know, he and I embraced for at least three minutes in absolute silence. He hugged me – a complete stranger! – and I heard the words of the Bible 'The love of God is shed abroad in your hearts' (Romans 5:5, KJV)!

'Dear brother,' I said to him. 'Jesus doesn't want you to do all this stuff. It will only harm you and these dear folks. Come let me pray for you. May I?'

He nodded in agreement.

'I'm going to ask the Lord Jesus to take your power away. Is that OK? Then you will know that he is the Lord.' And I prayed for him.

That was all! The Holy Spirit said that was all He wanted me to do, so I left telling the dear man that I would return the next time I was in Bushenyi because he would have a testimony to share.

It was interesting that the Holy Spirit said that that was enough, wasn't it? We evangelicals and charismatics would want to get him to 'sign on the dotted line', and follow the ritual of repeating the sinner's prayer, and then to teach him about the need for Bible study and church attendance, all which do have their place of course.

The second reason that I know there was an open heaven was now to be demonstrated. I continued on my journey back to the conference centre only to be dragged into a house by a woman pleading with me to tell them about Jesus. Within five minutes everyone in that household became born again and the woman's elderly mother who had been paralysed for fifteen years got up and danced with me. Praise God!

You see, what I am now about to describe will explain why the church in that city had been so divided and dysfunctional up until that conference.

We had been entering the city of Bushenyi some days earlier when a young English friend of mine, Ben Ward, who is currently living and ministering in Kabale, asked if we could stop and visit a pastor friend of his who lived near by. There was time before we went to the other side of the city to prepare the conference for the following day, so we parked the car and made our introductions.

The man was a bishop of a large group of churches and

welcomed us warmly until we explained our purpose in being in Bushenyi. 'No!' he said. He had not heard of the conference and had consequently no plans to attend. I urged him to accept our apologies for this oversight and to come none the less. Rather reluctantly he promised to reconsider.

We discovered later what had caused his embarrassment. In Bushenyi there were two very distinct groups of pastors, about twenty in each group, who had been at odds with each other because their spiritual fathers, now bishops, had not spoken for fifteen years after one had falsely accused the other of some misconduct.

The injured pastor was the host for the conference and we were now sitting in the very home of the man who was responsible for causing him such personal pain, and injury to the body of Christ. God moves in such sovereign ways doesn't he? We had no idea of all this at the time of course.

Apparently, the police had been sent in after the accusation and this had resulted in the pastor's imprisonment and torture. His young pregnant wife was also arrested and nearly lost the baby, and his family was destroyed. Two of his boys had become street children. Eventually, they were released but the relationship between them was never resolved nor the hurts healed. As a result the two groups of pastors under them felt 'orphaned'.

The bishop did come to the Body and the Bride conference and at the end of the four days, these two senior pastors were repenting and seeking forgiveness. Privately we took communion together and then ate a meal after which they addressed the conference assembly telling them what God had done. There was such rejoicing in Bushenyi and in the courts of heaven too I think. It was after this that we went on the march of declaration around the city and heaven came down to earth. 'Thy will be done on earth as it is in heaven'.

Open heaven? Yes, certainly, but at what cost? Unity through brokenness! That's the cost. There is no other way. Brokenness; because we owe everything to him!

God is calling out a new 'ecclesia' today: the 'called out ones' who will be totally dedicated to his service and to his glory. He is raising a new church, a new army of priests, warriors, and kings because they serve only the king.

The Bushenyi experience has proved to me that there are two things that are essential if true unity (and revival) is to be experienced in his church, and they must start amongst the leaders. First, heartfelt repentance for the divisiveness, pride, jealousy and isolationism that is in our hearts, and secondly a mindset change regarding territorial church and the acceptance of our corporate responsibility as leaders for that God-given territory. 'Leaders in any area,' he told me, when I sought him to define simply the difference between 'leaders' and 'leadership', move to 'leadership' when they accept their corporate responsibility for the territory I have given them'. His answer was so simple and so clear. Read it again and let it sink in! 'Leaders move from being 'leaders' to 'leadership' when they accept their corporate responsibility for the territory that I have given them'. That change of mindset will birth a new, united, vibrant and effective church.

May the Bushenyi experience be one we all long to see realized in our day and in our town and city. Do it again, Lord Jesus, and start in me!

Conclusion

Healing is one of the great signs of God's kingdom presence; it is one of the most tangible ways in which people encounter God and by which lives are changed. Don Latham's story, in chapter 2, illustrates the ripple effect that such signs can have in families and in communities. The three individual healing stories recorded in this chapter brought dramatic changes in people's lives: Nigel was effectively converted and then led into a powerful ministry; Wendy was converted and led on into a counselling ministry; Alice's healing and conversion were intertwined; Peter's discovery of the healing ministry helped to transform his parish; Howard's remarkable ministry opened up with a healing at his place of work and has lead him into a ministry where apostolic signs accompany his preaching.

Of course there is a deep mystery as to why and when healing takes place – the previous chapter, especially Walter Moberly's contribution, presents the other side of the coin [see also Liz Smith's poignant testimony at the end of the final chapter]; but where there is expectation and prevailing prayer, signs usually start to occur.

It is my belief that if churches would follow Peter Hancock's example, they would experience both numerical and spiritual growth.

Note

1 Augustine, *City of God*, book 22, chapters 8–10, translated by H. Bettenson, Penguin, 1984.

8

Jesus Brings Freedom

[Three stories from PNG (including David Lithgow*)/ Don and Heather McLean*/Dave Ridge*/Howard Barnes*/Suki Bright*/Lisa*/Anne Goode]

PAPUA NEW GUINEA IS AS DIFFERENT a country from the United Kingdom as it is possible to conceive. I want to begin this chapter with four stories from PNG and then show their surprising similarity with our situation. I visited PNG for the second time in 2005 to speak at the Wycliffe Bible translator's regional conference. It was very moving to meet a group of people so dedicated to translating the Scriptures and working in an environment that was difficult spiritually, socially and because of the climate. I was deeply impressed by the people that I met and fascinated by their stories which included spiritual battles and angelic protection amidst the everyday grind of spending up to fourteen years in a small community, translating the New Testament.

My first story was told me by a German missionary. He was living in a remote village in an Anglican mission area. He told how one evening his children woke up screaming. He was translating the New Testament in a difficult area where there was a lot of spiritual activity. He commanded whatever had entered their hut to leave in the name of Jesus. He was aware of a presence departing. Moments later, he heard a commotion amongst the animals of the village. This was followed by children crying. A few minutes later, down the valley in another village there was a repetition – first the animals and then the children cried.

This was one of a number of such experiences that this family endured. The missionary then commented to me, 'I couldn't tell this story in my home country.' 'Why?' I asked. 'Because no one would believe me – and they would probably stop funding me,' he replied sadly.

My second story concerns a missionary family who divided their time between a village, where they did translation work, and a house which they used as a base at the mission centre in Ukarumpa. Their son had told his parents that he had been troubled by a vision of a PNG man in his bedroom. When the mother shared this with their teenage daughter, who had gone through a difficult period at the mission school, Jessica said that she had had frightening experiences in her room for many years.

During the conference, the family asked Jane and me to come and pray. The children's rooms were on the ground floor. The house had been built into the side of a hill and so the ground floor had in reality been underground.

After prayer, we sensed that the house had been cleansed. The spiritual consequences were encouraging; very soon afterwards Jessica, who had been very questioning about Christianity told her parents that she had become a Christian and she was baptized by immersion in the nearby river.

I don't know why the children had the problem in their rooms. The Ukarumpa mission site was built on land which had been the warring field between the two people groups who lived in the area. It is possible that the house was built on a site where there had been battles and cannibalism.

My third story is taken from the biography of **David Lithgow**[1]. He was a famous translator who spent much of his life in the Woodlark islands – a small group of islands a few miles north of PNG. He was brought up as a Bible-believing Christian, he qualified as a doctor, and dedicated his life to making a number of New Testament translations for different language groups in the area.

Late in his life, he encountered the renewal movement. Soon afterwards, a patient whom he had diagnosed as mentally deranged committed suicide. David was sure that he had been demon-possessed and that he had failed to realize this. He started to speak out against *tamudumudulele*, which was the local word for satanic power. The people, including many church leaders, as it turned out, relied on magic for the protection of their crops and release and protection from disease. Many of the leaders were terrified when he started to speak out. But gradually they saw some powerful deliverance from evil spirits and some dramatic healings. Gradually the church leaders were won over.

One Sunday in a small village, David spoke about magic and sorcery, urging people to forsake these practices. As he sat down to pray, he heard the sound of footsteps coming down the aisle of the church, stopping in a solid block in front of the pulpit. When he looked up, most of the older men were standing round him, many of them church leaders. Some even had their magic tools with them – wood, gum, ginger, stones and bones – all of which were eagerly handed over.

The result was a huge fire later in the day on the beach. As in Ephesus (see Acts 19) huge quantities of spirit paraphernalia were committed to the flames. This was followed by the baptism of sixteen adults in the warm sea!

Such occurrences were common at the end of David's ministry. The islands which had been nominally Christian for seventy years experienced renewal, freedom and revival!

What relevance has all this to our situation? A great deal,
I believe. The first story illustrates our need to speak out
about these matters without fear or favour. With my friend's
permission, I retold his story to the conference adding that
they must tell their home churches about these matters.
Western Christendom desperately needs to be reminded of
the spiritual battle. I have witnessed similar phenomena after
prayer in both Africa and rural Somerset.[2] We, who have
been privileged to minister in these areas, must speak out
and tell the good news that risen Jesus Christ has defeated
the powers of darkness (see Colossians 2:15 and the whole of
Mark's Gospel).

The second story could be repeated many times in the
UK. I have prayed in houses, stables and a factory with similar results. Even as I write, I am preparing to visit another
house where a fringe member of my church has discerned
that a friend has a serious problem. This will be a double
evangelistic opportunity both to the fringe church member
with some psychic awareness and her troubled friend.

People in troubled buildings need our help. It is a wonderful opportunity to present the gospel and can often lead to
conversions. If we are not able to help they will turn to psychic and spiritualist healers with results that are spiritually
dubious and financially costly. I am amazed how many people in inner Leicester have troubled houses, troubled neighbours or who when bereaved turn to the dubious comfort of
the spiritualists.

The third story illustrates what happens when an area
experiences real renewal. We must go out proclaiming the
power of the Holy Spirit and expecting signs of healing,
deliverance, conversion and social change to follow.

My fourth deliverance encounter is also supplied by some
friends that I met in PNG.

* * *

Don and Heather McLean *have been working in translation and literacy with SIL [Wycliffe Bible translators] in the
Western Highlands Province of PNG since 2001. They spent
several years in other areas of the country, when their children were younger.*

In the early 1980s, we lived at Telefomin in the Western Sepik
Province of Papua New Guinea. We were working with the
Australian Baptist Missionary Society, in an area which was
renowned for worshipping a very powerful spirit goddess,
Afek. There was a particularly well-known 'man house' not
far from the mission houses that tourists were very keen to
visit. No national women were permitted to go anywhere
near the area, but at that time we were terribly naïve about
the spirit world which is involved in Animism and would
sometimes allow our two young daughters to take visitors to
the area to see the outside of the house. They would have
been about ten and eight years old at the time. Although still
inexperienced in this spiritual world, I would feel a 'creepy'
sensation if I ever ventured into the area, even with a group
of other people. My husband said that I imagined it, but I
knew otherwise.

Several years later, at our home church back in Australia,
when our spiritual eyes had been somewhat opened, a visiting pastor asked any of the congregation who had been missionaries to come forward so that he could pray for us in
relation to the dark side of the spirit realm with which we
had no doubt had some contact. I turned to my older daughter and asked her to accompany her sister, brother and parents to the front, to which she tacitly replied, 'There is

nothing wrong with me!' The look in her eyes told me something else. Our pastor told us that if she had been in rebellion against us on any of those visits near the spirit house, then there would have been an open door for any of those dark spirits to enter her life.

Our older daughter had returned with us from Papua New Guinea when she was nearly twelve. She seemed to think that she had missed out on a lot of activities and pleasures that her peer group had experienced by that time and set about catching up with them. No amount of counsel or warning could change her downward path. She told us that she would not learn by anything other than her own experience. That is what happened and she was badly burned by those experiences for many years. I had had a very legalistic upbringing which I did not find easy to abandon. They were tumultuous years for the whole family.

After our older daughter left home, we were sometimes able to communicate more effectively. Occasionally I mentioned that her acting as a tour guide to the spirit house back in Telefomin may have had an adverse spiritual effect on her life. She listened, but would never let us pray for her close up and definitely not allow us to touch her while we prayed. She often used to remind us of the times people had told her as a little girl that they believed that God had a very special purpose for her life and would ask plaintively why everything completely opposite seemed to be dominant in her life. She had a broken engagement followed by a broken marriage and she spiralled deeper into depression and a life out of control.

She was a wonderful, caring palliative care nurse by this time, but was no longer able to function in that capacity. We tried everything that we could think of to help her physically and spiritually, but the more we tried, it seemed the worse she became and we were finally advised to just keep on loving her but leave everything else in God's hands. We had asked many people to join us in praying for her desperate situation. Her paternal grandmother was probably one of the most fervent pray-ers for her beloved grandaughter's deliverance. At times our daughter would seek secular counselling, but always resisted any suggestions that she needed to see a Christian counsellor.

When our other two children had left home and started on their career paths, we began training with Wycliffe Bible Translators. We were finally ready to leave and returned to Papua New Guinea in the year 2000 with the blessing of all the children. Our older daughter's comment was, 'I knew that you would go back one day.'

During our early years back in the country, we became aware of a nationwide prayer movement called Operation Joshua. One of the results of this movement was a request from the people of Telefomin for someone to destroy the old spirit house nearby. It was falling into disrepair and the people themselves were becoming frightened of the building and what it had stood for. The leader of Operation Joshua was very happy to oblige and started a fire which destroyed the decaying building for ever. At that time, most of the local people were delighted, but more recent reports indicate that if the man who headed Operation Joshua returned to the area, there are some who would willingly take his life.

In Papua New Guinea, from time to time we were able to speak on the phone with our children when we visited a nearby Bible College. At that time we were living in a very primitive village setting with no facilities of our own. Just over two years ago, I was talking on the phone with our older daughter when she told me that she had recently asked a lady from a nearby church whether or not she could have been affected by those times of taking people to visit the area of the spirit house.

This spiritually sensitive lady said, 'Oh my dear, let me pray for you!' Miracle number one was that she allowed this lady to pray for her and no doubt she touched our daughter while praying. Miracle number two was that for some time our daughter's sleeping pattern improved noticeably. After her marriage broke down, she had not been able to sleep at night and so slept a lot of the following seven years away.

We believe that the burning of that spirit house way up north in the depths of Papua New Guinea, actually broke the spiritual bondage in our daughter's life and for the first time she was free to ask for spiritual help for her complex problems. This was only the beginning, and there were still many hard times ahead for her.

In the year 2004, three of our close family members died within three months of one another. We returned from Papua New Guinea and were able to be with each member in their last stages of illness. Our daughter was present at two out of the three funerals. At the last one, my ninety-six-year-old mother's, our daughter became distraught. She could not understand why, as she had never felt particularly close to my mother. She realized that she had not forgiven her maternal grandmother for the way that she had brought up me, her mother, so legalistically. By this time my relationship with my daughter had become much closer. But, although a committed Christian from the age of nine, until I was in my early forties I had not discovered the freedom of grace. I had passed many rules and regulations on to my own children, contributing to many of our hard family situations.

Many years ago, my mother had requested that one of my

cousins who is a pastor, conduct her funeral service. He gave a beautifully simple gospel message at the funeral chapel. When he saw our daughter's distress, he asked her if she would like to visit some ladies at his church where she could receive some counsel. She agreed but approximately five more months went by before she managed to get herself to the church.

We had returned to Papua New Guinea by this time. She told me on the phone that she was deeply touched by the lovely caring ladies who led her to renounce all kinds of behaviour which she knew had kept her from receiving the release for which she had been longing. She started to read Rick Warren's book, *The Purpose-Driven Life*, with a real fervour, looking up every reference in three or four different versions of the Bible so that she could glean every ounce of meaning out of them. She felt that the Lord was speaking directly to her and started to mould her life on the wisdom that she was reading.

One day in February 2005, on the same day that a devastating flood had forced us to leave our village house and move to some premises of the nearby Bible College, we received a fax from her saying that she had given up smoking and was going to be baptized by immersion the following Sunday, at the church which she had been attending regularly for some months. She hoped that we would understand that she couldn't wait for us to come home in September that year, but felt that she must obey the Lord straight away. Of course we were delighted and arranged for several friends to stand in for us and witness this wonderful step that she was about to take. She was now nearly thirty-three years of age.

From that time, she has gone on from strength to strength, telling others freely about the goodness of God to her. She delights to study the Word of God with a large concordance that we were delighted to give her. Her television viewing and music choices have changed dramatically and she has destroyed many things around her home which she felt were not advantageous to her Christian walk.

She did a course called 'Cleansing Streams' recently and sent a letter to many of her friends, including us, inviting us to tell her frankly any character defects which we might have noticed in her. This is a far cry from that time when she brusquely stated, 'There's nothing wrong with me!' She has become fascinated by stories of those who have been prepared to give their lives in martyrdom rather than deny their Lord, and said, 'I want to be strong enough to do the same, should my turn come.'

What a wonderful change has taken place in her life! We are constantly amazed and continually grateful when we see what she is allowing the Lord to do in her life. If I mention to her that a certain person has been praying for her for many years, she always asks me to thank them for their faithfulness. She has stated to us 'You must have been praying for me for so long. I'm so sorry that I couldn't do it for you, but when God told me to change my self-destructive habits, I had to obey!'

Is it any wonder that we are so grateful to our Lord?

*   *   *

Dave Ridge *(see also chapter 5) has accompanied me on a number of missions. This experience with a different team in Nigeria is a powerful illustration of how healing takes place when Satan's influence is rejected (see Luke 13:10–17).*

In January 2005 I went as part of a team of five to Nigeria to teach at a conference for clergy. There were about 200 ordained and lay leaders attending the week-long conference. It was a packed programme and we only had only one slot in the schedule to pray for physical healing for those who wanted it. As in any country where access to medical care is costly, if available at all, when we asked those who needed physical healing to come forward, almost every one of those present came forward.

This meant that each member of the team had more than thirty people to pray for, so the approach I took was simply to ask each person what the problem was and pray that Jesus would heal them and then pray for the next person. I guess I gave each person about thirty seconds.

The next day a man, aged about fifty, came up to me saying that his foot had been healed when I had prayed for him. I didn't even remember praying for him let alone that it was his foot! I said something along the lines of how pleased I was for him but he was very excited and wanted to tell me more. So I arranged to see him later with one of the local team to help me as the man's English was not good.

When we met up his story was something like this. As a young boy he had been initiated into a secret society against his will. An occult ceremony was held by his uncle which culminated with some powder being placed into his hand which suddenly and apparently by the powers of darkness burst into flames. He, not surprisingly, tipped the powder out of his hand onto the floor and put out the flames by stamping on it with his feet which were bare. He was told that a curse had been placed upon him so that if he ever renounced the secret society or told anyone about this ceremony he would die, and so had lived in fear ever since. From that time on the foot that had stamped out the flames was apparently somewhat crippled. It was much more than a simple burn which would have healed in time.

So it was decades later, by which time he was an ordained minister, that he came for prayer for his foot – without even mentioning the history. But Jesus healed it and then he knew at last that the curse had been broken. Together we were able to pray that he would be free of this bondage to exercise his ministry as God intended. He showed me his foot as proof of the healing – of course I had not seen the 'before' picture and I was amazed at how flat his foot was, he had no instep but this is normal for someone who walks everywhere they go! He testified before people who knew him that he had run up the hill by his house the morning after the healing, which he had not been able to do before.

*   *   *

Howard Barnes *(for a brief biography see page 167) wrote me this account of deliverance ministry in Africa. His emphasis on a gentle approach is so important – so much ministry, especially in Africa, is accompanied by shouting, screaming, and in some extreme cases physical violence by the ministry team. He writes:*

In my walk with the Lord over the years I have discovered that there has been so much additional pain caused to already hurting people by those who, in ignorance and with over-enthusiasm, have tried to minister deliverance to the demon-oppressed or possessed. My experience in Africa has highlighted this situation very clearly and through it, as I sought the Lord for a better way, a 'Christ-like' way, He showed me some things that would radically change my ministry in this needy area. I had always been concerned by the amount of noise and energy displayed by some, especially in Africa, engaged in deliverance, since I did not see Jesus working this way.

At the beginning of 2003, before the birth of HfCNM (see page 167), I was working in Malawi, Central Africa, at the invitation of Archbishop Harry Kaitano, overseer of the African International Church in that country. I had previously been ordained a bishop and later an apostle to that church throughout Africa, but I had accepted it 'only for a season' – God's season, and they had agreed. I was happy to serve in that capacity since I could see the amazing transformation that was taking place in the AIC, under Harry's leadership. He had brought this traditional African church into renewal.

Harry had invited me to preach at a series of services and crusades throughout Malawi. We based ourselves in the interior villages; many thousand were saved during that month's mission, and awesome miracles took place. One open-air Sunday morning service in particular remains etched in my memory. It taught me so much about God's offer of 'gentle deliverance' for the possessed.

We had planned to preach in the compound area of a large Presbyterian church, but for some reason, although this had been well planned, it had become impossible. So, very hurriedly, we had to rethink. Jesus opened up to us an opportunity to go into an interior village the other side of the new dam. That Sunday morning over 2,500 people turned up (news had spread by bush telegraph!) and after preaching, 1,000 people were saved and mighty miracles were done in his name. The first people to be kneeling in front of the huge crowd to receive Jesus were the chief of that village and his four elders.

We had taken with us about twenty pastors from the African International Churches in that region and after an early seminar before the main service, where we taught them about praying for the sick, we moved into the morning service.

It was great to bring them out to minister and to pray for the sick, as many of them had never ventured out in faith before. The blind saw, the deaf heard. The Lord confirmed his word with the 'signs and wonders' promised. I would pray alongside one priest or bishop and anoint the sick person with oil and then see them instantly healed. I would then encourage that bishop to do the same over the next person in the line. To see them surprised and blessed by the fruit of their prayers was truly awesome. The service was followed by a celebration of spontaneous praise, worship and dancing!

At the end of the two or three hours of what I can only describe as a party, the village mad woman arrived in rags and filth. People began to respond as she acted out her total madness in front of them causing them to laugh at her as we in the West often do at the antics of a drunkard. I was angry with their response, so angry that the 'Lion of Judah' roared within me. I told the people, 'Sit down and pray for her! She was one of God's lost ones.' With a word of rebuke to the demon, the woman was thrown to the ground and the crowd hushed.

Now, God does not want any drama or hysterics. Demons love to draw attention to themselves, especially if they anticipate a defeat, and then they will want to harm the person in some way if they can. Jesus never allowed it! So, I knelt down beside the unconscious woman and whispered in her ear, speaking to the demon, 'The blood of Jesus comes between you and this woman. The blood of Jesus sets her free. Go in the name of Jesus! You can stay there if you wish but the blood of Jesus comes against you and it will burn you!' With that the demon immediately left her with a sigh. I heard it leave from her ear like a tyre deflating suddenly and she was free!

I noticed she had witchcraft bracelets on her arm and legs and I called for a knife but to no avail. So, I bit several off with my teeth and held them up directly in front of her eyes commanding that she regain consciousness. I bit off another and another.

'See, Jesus sets you free!' I cried. With a shout of 'Jesus!' the woman now began to take them off, tearing at them one by one until they were all gone. Then she knelt down and in her right mind she received Jesus as her Lord and saviour. We silenced the crowd so they could hear her confession and witness this transformation. Two young girls in the choir offered some of their own clothes and the women took off her filthy rags and got dressed, now made whole in every way! Praise him!

* * *

Suky Bright *is much involved with all aspects of prayer in Leicester. She is on the leadership of 'Watchman on the Walls', a 24/7 city-wide prayer initiative, and also 'Prayer for Israel'. As part of a small team, Suky researches and prays, as the Holy Spirit directs, into the history of Leicester and its effect on the city's present condition and has seen remarkable changes.*

Together with her husband, Graham, Suky has been a

member of Bible Hall Fellowship, Highfields, since 1979 and is part of the leadership team.

The story begins in 1976 with the death of my son Luke, aged four and a half months. At the time of his death my husband and I were young Christians but, at this most tragic of times, we both felt and knew the arms and comfort of the Lord our God. I experienced for myself the 'everlasting arms of comfort and love' upholding and supporting me through a grief that is indescribable in its pain and loss.

After a few months we were expecting another baby – the mixture of excitement, guilt and fear carried on throughout my pregnancy, but when Matthew was born it was wonderful. However, unknown to us, some of our friends were spiritualists and had, on the night of Luke's death, 'seen' him die. They did not reveal this to us until one night when Matthew was three months old. I was on my own with the woman (all this was staged so I would be alone with her whilst her husband took mine out) when she said she had a message from Luke! At first I was really scared by this, but she assured me it was OK. Not understanding the Scriptures or being aware of the wiles of the wicked one, I allowed her to tell me what Luke's message was. After she had told me, I was quite happy and somewhat relieved – for about five minutes that is! Once I had got home and the realization hit me of what had just taken place I was filled with fear and apprehension.

From that time on I was so afraid to get out of the bed in the dark to feed Matthew and had to have the lights on everywhere I went – I was scared that Luke would appear to me in the night and I begged the Lord not to allow this. My husband was dismissive of my fear and dread – he showed no signs of being disturbed – perhaps because he was not the recipient of the 'message'. Sadly, after another year, my marriage came to an end and I moved back to Leicester, but the fear and the dread dogged my life for the next fifteen years.

In 1982 I remarried and had three more children – all strapping lads and all committed Christians! However, this 'curse' as I felt it had become continued to haunt me. When my youngest son developed acute asthma and was in and out of hospital with alarming regularity during the first two years of his life, I was convinced he would die – after all the Lord could take any of my children at any time – he took Luke, didn't he?

I started to see a psychologist but without success. I thought that this was my lot in life and I would just have to suffer this as part of my walk as a Christian! I was given advice by a well-meaning church friend who counselled, 'Don't ask why, dear, just say, "Yes, Lord!"' which is what I did with my lips, but my heart was screaming out for answers! Why did you take him? What was the point? Why didn't you heal him of his brain tumour? Why have you left me in such pain? I want my son back! It was some years later when the realization dawned on me that it was OK to ask why.

Many people in the Scriptures, especially in the psalms, asked God hard questions and they never got hit by a thunderbolt! So I did start asking why. I didn't get any answers but the relief of just getting these questions off my chest was considerable!

A further three years passed. One summer we all went to a Christian camp – a place I definitely did not want to go to! Far too many 'hallelujah sisters' for my liking, but I went along. We were around the communal cocoa table one evening when I made a chance remark about being given a message by a medium some years before. Immediately a wonderful Christian brother was alerted in the spirit at what I said and with his wife and my sister set about delivering me from this dreadful curse I had been subjected to for so many years.

He guided me through prayer after prayer, confessing, repenting and receiving! The night was dark and cloudless with a myriad of stars across the black sky; the wind gained in its intensity, and at one time became so ferocious we feared we would all be swept away. It was actually a very hostile wind which we all felt was an enemy attack but to no avail. That night I received a glorious deliverance from all my fears and I experienced the great forgiveness and grace of God. I went back to my tent and shared all this with the family. During the night I needed to go outside – something I always dreaded in the dark – but as I went I didn't seem to have the same fear as normal. As I got out into the field where the toilet tent was I saw the most beautiful sight ever. The night was just beginning to give way to the dawn. High in the dark sky the deep blue velvet was gradually giving way to the cobalt blue horizon.

The earth was as quiet as could be – I felt that I was the only one awake! There in the sky was the most perfect crescent moon accompanied by the bright, morning star! I gasped in absolute wonder at this magnificent canvas – it was as if the Lord had painted it just for me – and then I heard the Lord say to me 'Suky, this is the first day of your new life.' The words were so clear and so personal and he even spoke my name. He was indeed my 'morning star'!

The following year we went back to the Christian camp. One evening we were being encouraged to give all our hurts, pain and anything else that was 'hanging on in there' that shouldn't be. I gladly gave all my tears and pain for Luke over to the Lord, and as I did so, it felt to me as though a bird flew away from my heart. I was overwhelmed at the release! There went all that pain. Later on in the week I stood up in response to the call to commit myself to pray for my own city. A novel thought! After this defining week, not only for me but for the whole family, my sister and her family, the Lord started to radically change our ideas. Our fellowship began to change – we were liberated! New things began to happen at Bible Hall.

Moving on to the late 1990s; I went with a few other ladies to a 'Women of Promise' day near Newark. The venue was an imposing Victorian country house with high ceilings and lush furnishings. As we stepped into the conference room I spotted a work of art, painted by one of the conference organizers, placed very high on the wall just in front of me. I was glued to it – couldn't take my eyes of what I saw! The painting was of a broken heart – made from chains – with a dove flying out from it – released and free!

I gasped 'Lord! Look! This painting is just like my heart was until the day I released all my pain to you!' The Lord said, 'No, Suky, that was the day I put my Holy Spirit within you!' It all made such beautiful sense. I wept and wept with gratitude to the Lord who noticed me, forgave, healed and restored my life so that I could serve him.

I don't know why it took fifteen years for me to be released from my fears but I do know that Jesus is my deliverer, redeemer, restorer, liberator, healer and wonderful Lord. Now I serve him in Leicester as part of the 'Prayer for Leicester' initiative. I am, along with my husband Graham, part of the leadership team at Bible Hall Fellowship.

* * *

One Thursday afternoon, I received an urgent call from some clergy who were struggling to pray with a woman who appeared to be demonized. She was sitting in the downstairs cloakroom hissing and speaking in strange tongues. Today, **Lisa** *is a working mother who is very involved in her local church. She is hoping, in the years ahead, to serve God in a full-time capacity. This is her own account of what happened.*

In November 2004, I experienced what it was like to be possessed by an evil spirit and to speak in demonic tongues. At the very mention of Jesus' name, I was in pain and I could not bear to look at a cross. Apparently when people tried to help me I either hissed at them or spoke in demonic tongues. Although this time in my life was very frightening, I clung onto my faith and put my total trust in God. I prayed that He would bring me through this crisis. The love that I felt for God, and my heart and soul that I had given to Jesus Christ, was crying out to God to deliver me from the powers of darkness.

Eventually, I came out of the small room where I had been hiding and talked to someone who had come to help me. He led me through some prayers of renunciation and repentance; eventually anointing me with oil. I felt much better and freer (although I had one period about a year later when the demonic tongues reappeared and I needed more prayer).

I was delivered from the evil power and set free to love and adore my God. God was truly glorified throughout. All who there experienced his power and his mercy; we were all given a new infilling of the Holy Spirit.

As Christians, we are each on a journey with God. We will

each have experiences which will help to develop and grow in Christ.

Some things we may never understand. For instance, no one was sure why I had this problem. I had a very minor experience of the occult some years earlier as a teenager; I was also under some strong emotional pressure at the time (the unwanted attention of a fellow worshipper).

If no one is clear as to why this problem occurred, there is no doubting the remarkable change in Lisa's personality. She has become much more confident, has a considerable gift of discernment for other people, has seen her husband come to faith and be confirmed, and is hoping to serve God in a wider ministry. The relapse which she refers to above is instructive.

I should have prayed more on the first occasion. She still had an ability to speak in tongues and it wasn't until she asked me to listen to this that it became apparent there was a further need for ministry. Although her reaction to prayer was very dramatic (she was crawling around my study floor hissing at her vicar and myself) the period of prayer was quite short. At the end, she was very peaceful. Since then we have met regularly and I can only marvel at her steady growth in maturity and discipleship.

Lisa concludes with a personal reflection:

But I am content to rest in the certainty that God is our creator, a loving Father whose son Jesus took our flesh, and he is my Lord and saviour. Each day, as we wake in his presence, we can put on the full armour of God. We know that he is with us through all things and that he has carved each of us out on the palm of his hand. He will not forget us (see Isaiah 49:15); but we must be on our guard because the devil comes in many forms and disguises. We have absolute assurance of God's protection and the apostle John gives us this promise: 'You, dear children, are from God and have overcome them, because the one who is in you is greater than the one who is in the world' (1 John 4:4). Alleluia!

Here today in the death of Christ we live and in the power of Christ we stand firm and faithful.

* * *

Anne Goode *was my friend for many years; she used to attend our church and was very involved in prayer and witness to those who attended the Glastonbury Festival. Many weary travellers received refreshment, and the offer of a Gideon Bible, at a gate in her field which was just by one of the entrances to the Festival. Early in her time in Somerset, she was troubled by her buildings.*

I had just moved to Somerset. We had bought an overpriced attractive eighteenth-century building which was immediately opposite the site of an annual pop festival which was growing in international importance. I was aware of an atmosphere of menace which was affecting my family. My academically brilliant husband began behaving oddly, displaying signs of early dementia; my musically gifted son was being bullied at school; my daughter spent all her time like a ghost child, pale and withdrawn, in the stables; and I was prone to uncontrollable outbursts of rage which upset the whole family.

In spiritual and emotional disarray, I sought the help of John Woolmer whose recently published book, *Growing up to Salvation*, contained a chapter about the occult which I read with surprise and relief. During prayer, which included the laying on of hands, I experienced liquid light flowing through my whole body. I found that I was totally free of the dark fear which had gripped every area of my life. Problems within the house still needed dealing with, but I was no longer afraid and family life improved. The church began to use the house for staff days, but I sensed that the house needed deeper ministry than the simple blessing that had been given to it.

After the mysterious death in the field of one of my daughter's horses, John decided, during a staff day, to perform a full-scale exorcism of the whole premises, complete with a large jug of holy water (water that had been set aside by prayer for this purpose). My daughter and I were particularly troubled by unpleasant graffiti on the stable walls which seemed to imply somewhat sinister use by previous occupants. I felt that the evil presence had been around the buildings for a long time.

The staff team eventually gathered around the stable which had been previously occupied by the dead horse, and they stood in a semi-circle. John entered the stables, prayed in tongues, and tipped half a jug of water on the straw, commanding any evil presence to leave in the name of Jesus. One of the staff members, not used to this sort of thing, visibly jumped backwards and described how a huge force leaving the stables seemed to hit him at the moment of the prayer. The results of the prayer were beneficial. Visitors, and there are many of them, invariably comment on the peace and beauty of the place.

I was quite sceptical at the time, but saw the dramatic effect on my praying partner Albert as the force left the stable. All that happened about twenty years ago, and Anne remained a good friend until her peaceful and quite remarkable death in 2004. She suffered from an unpleasant form of cancer, but was wonderfully looked after by her family and church, and died in her sleep on Christmas night, twenty-four hours after attending the midnight communion in the church I used to lead.

Conclusion

There is no rational explanation for these things. In rural Zambia I even heard a spirit speak through a local woman speaking in perfect Oxbridge English. The spirit said, 'Go away, I am not leaving this person!' In Oxford, a Guyanese teenager was lying on a couch. My rector, Michael Green, and I had been asked to pray with her. As we approached a voice spoke through her 'You lot are a load of bumbling amateurs!' These events are explicable only by reading and believing the Gospels. Jesus' presence (for instance in Mark 1:23–26) often provoked this sort of reaction; prayers offered in his name can have the same effect today.

It is also important to realize that the phenomena associated with these sorts of problems are identical in sophisticated Oxford and rural Zambia. This should dispose of the sceptical view that these things only occur in cultures that expect them!

It is also remarkable how often physical healing, and a general sense of well-being, follows deliverance. Peter Hancock and I noticed this in Zambia (see page 163); Dave Ridge (above) saw this in Nigeria and Lisa (above) certainly experienced this.

These sorts of encounters are rare; there is a regrettable tendency in some Christian circles to attribute almost any strange behaviour or illness to the devil. This leads to attempted exorcisms of non-existent spirits and to pastoral chaos which causes as much harm as the denial that such an approach is ever valid.

Finally, I would say that these spiritual encounters are powerful evidence for the power and presence of the risen Lord. To feel a physical force leaving some stables doesn't happen in normal circumstances! If an evil power wasn't present and if Christ did not rise from the dead; these kinds of prayers would be an absurd waste of time and completely ineffective. In each case, they brought a swift transformation to troubled situations. Consequently, they provide glorious back-up evidence for the historicity of the resurrection and the spiritual reality of the encounters in these and other chapters.

Notes

1 Lynette James *Not in the Common Mould – the life of Dr David Lithgow*, Wycliffe Media
2 See John Woolmer, *Healing and Deliverance*, Monarch, 1999, for many examples in England and abroad; see also *Angels of Glory and Darkness*, Monarch, 2006, especially page 15.

9

The Holy Spirit Transforms

[Andrew Watson*/Michael Wenham*/Betty Craig*/Liz Smith*]

IN THIS CHAPTER, I HAVE INCLUDED four testimonies. In each of them the key experience seems to have been an overwhelming encounter with the Holy Spirit. For Andrew, the sudden gift of tongues was part of a remarkable weekend which transformed a tough youth group. For Michael, a dry, tired ministry was set alight and, much later, he was able to cope with the onset of motor neurone disease with amazing calm. For Betty, a totally unexpected encounter as she prayed after reading a book led on to an effective ministry in the local parish church. For Liz, the power of the Holy Spirit swept away her convinced cynicism and unbelief. Later on, this gave her enough faith to cling onto God and to cry out for help after a terrible tragedy within the family.

The experience of being continuously 'filled with the Spirit' (Ephesians 5:18) is experienced gently and gradually by some; for others it happens with an overwhelming suddenness. Two personal experiences from nature can illustrate the difference.

Our family had a number of summer holidays at Roquebrune sur Orb in the South of France. The Orb is a gentle river. Swimming was safe and enjoyable; but around midday we had to take extra care. About ten kilometres upstream, in mid-morning, a power station disgorged a lot of water which increased the current quite dramatically. The river was still safe, but when the water reached Roquebrune the flow of the river had become much more powerful.

I would compare that experience with a gradual infilling of the Holy Spirit. The change in the current was imperceptible but after a while it was undeniable. When we are gradually filled by the Holy Spirit, the effect is very similar.

Rather more dramatic was some work that I did in the school nature reserve at Winchester. Each autumn, stagnant foetid ditches were mud-scooped by a group of rather unwilling boys who were doing this work as an alternative to military activities in the corps. The effect was fairly minimal, not unlike some renewal programmes in churches.

One afternoon, the boys suggested that we cut a channel back to a fast-flowing stream which went around the edge of the reserve. This would divert water down our ditch and back into the stream. It involved many afternoons of hard work cutting through a chalk bank and then digging a channel across a marshy swamp. Eventually, the connection was made and the last blocking clod of earth removed.

The water poured through, the ditch was transformed. Two hours later, it had a clean chalk base with a fine trout swimming up it. I remember talking about this at a conference. I said that 'being filled with the Spirit' was not an optional extra but a military command. A man in the audience, an army officer, sat bolt upright and almost saluted. He appeared to have been somewhat uninterested in the week-long conference; but now he was alert. He received prayer. I met him years later and he described it as a transforming experience.

Always, there seems to be great fruit in worship, evangelism and in a new openness to the gifts of the Holy Spirit.

Many people then come to understand God as their Father (see especially Romans 8:14–17). This greater intimacy with a God, who is both personal and ever present, leads to a much greater confidence in matters spiritual.

The Toronto experience in the 1990s was quite controversial. However both Andrew and Liz were helped by it; as were many others. The outpouring of the Holy Spirit at the Toronto airport church made a wonderful difference to the confidence and spiritual maturity of many people.

The ditch illustration does carry one warning. Years later, in a very dry summer, I went back to admire my handiwork. I was very disappointed. The ditch was almost dry and was reduced to a few pools of water. It is possible to be greatly renewed by the Holy Spirit and then to lose much of the benefit. St Paul's words (Ephesians 5:18) are best translated 'be continuously filled with the Spirit'. At the end of the chapter, I will consider how we might make a response to these testimonies.

* * *

Andrew Watson *became a Christian during a revival at Winchester College in the 1970s (see chapter 3, and Richard Harvey's testimony in chapter 1). He is now the vicar of St Stephen's, Twickenham, a large and flourishing church which has successfully 'planted' new congregations in the surrounding area.*

I became a committed Christian at the age of thirteen, during an extraordinary time of revival in my school. At one point thirty boys (out of fifty) in my house were reading the Bible and praying together on a weekly basis – and many of those thirty have gone on to become church ministers and evangelists.

In those early days I was very conscious of God's presence with me. I remember a talk on the cross given by an elderly clergyman which moved me to tears; and many a walk beside the River Itchen where I sensed the 'still, small voice' of God's Spirit encouraging and directing me.

My later teenage years and early twenties were more of a struggle. I never turned my back on God. I even co-led the Christian Union in my college at Cambridge. But somehow the spirituality which had so nurtured my early days as a Christian seemed inadequate to the new challenges I was beginning to face.

In particular, the possibility of encountering or experiencing God was treated with some suspicion in the Christian circles in which I was then moving. A friend, who'd been a fellow bassoon player in the National Youth Orchestra in our early teens, got involved in a rather extreme Pentecostal group at that time: and his increasingly eccentric antics (including regular shouts of 'Praise the Lord!' in the middle of our rather formal college dinners) seemed to confirm that those suspicions were justified!

Two incidents (at much the same time) shook me out of my spiritual apathy. One was the dramatic healing of a close friend of mine, a cellist who was severely epileptic. That encounter is her story, not mine. The other was an unforgettable series of events in a windswept Yorkshire youth centre, which were little short of miraculous.

By this time I had left university, and was working as a caretaker and youth worker in North London. My caretaking duties were mundane, and something of a shock after the rarefied atmosphere of the Cambridge Law Library and

Corpus Christi Chapel. My youth-working duties were emotionally draining, periodically terrifying, and apparently fruitless in any obvious sense. Indeed the youth club itself, though hugely popular in the area, had seen very little by way of evangelistic fruit during the ten years in which it had been running.

A youth club holiday was planned, based in the Yorkshire Dales – and I, along with the rest of the youth team, had been praying that this would mark a turning point in the spiritual temperature of the club. We were particularly excited about the Wednesday night, when we'd invited a guest speaker to join us – someone who had worked with Jackie Pullinger in her extraordinary ministry to drug addicts out in Hong Kong.

To say that the holiday got off to a bad start would be an understatement! One of the minibuses broke down before we'd even left Islington, and the young people spent most of that Sunday sitting around my flat, chain-smoking and getting more and more fed up. Eventually the problem was fixed and we set off, arriving in Yorkshire in the late evening. The young people – fearless in their own urban environment – found the quietness and solitude of the youth centre almost unbearable, and were particularly unnerved when they discovered it had previously been an abbey. The 'ghosts' may have been real or imagined, but the youngsters' fear made for a sleepless night.

The next day went from bad to worse. A group of young people made their way down to the (rather civilized) local pub, where they proceeded to beat up one of the regulars. Ronnie, the ringleader, promised he'd be back the next day to trash the place.

That evening, when we'd finally got the young people settled, the youth leaders gathered to pray – and in sheer desperation we ended up praying all night! The next morning our prayers were partially answered as Ronnie woke up with a splitting headache, and spent the following twenty-four hours in bed! But it was on the Wednesday that God intervened most wonderfully.

A couple of hours before our guest speaker arrived; I managed to spend some time alone on a beautiful hill overlooking the youth centre. I was praying, and bringing to God my sense of spiritual dryness. Then I found myself running out of English words and starting to speak in a language I didn't know. I'd read about this 'speaking in tongues' before, but had never experienced it. In some sense it seemed remarkably normal, surprisingly so. But as my prayer time came to an end I knew that something had changed: that my spiritual drought (which had lasted the best part of five years) had come to an end.

That evening we managed to herd the young people into the meeting room, where our guest speaker prepared to address us. My first impressions of the lady were hardly positive. She was late middle-aged, grey-haired and very softly spoken, and I feared that our teenagers would make mincemeat of the poor woman!

But as she began to speak, an extraordinary calm enveloped the room. I don't remember much of what was said, though I think it was mainly a series of testimonies to God's faithfulness among the triad gangs of Hong Kong. What I do remember was a powerful experience of God's Spirit, drawing us all into his presence.

I looked round, and Ronnie was in tears. So were many of the others. When the lady finally finished; she invited people to see her personally if they'd like to become Christians, and a queue of thirty-five young people stood patiently for up to an hour, waiting to respond!

Those youngsters all gave their lives to Christ that night – and they all received the gift of tongues. For them 'tongues' gave them a language with which to pray (something they'd never done before), as well as demonstrating to them the reality of what had happened to them. Over the next three months, forty more young people became Christians in and around the Islington youth club. The testimony (and transformation) of people like Ronnie was simply irresistible.

After Islington I returned to Cambridge for my theological training, and met my future wife at a Rowan Williams lecture on Origen! I was duly ordained and served a curacy in the West Midlands before we moved to London, to take up an exciting new post in Notting Hill.

It was during that time that the so-called 'Toronto Blessing' hit churches all round the country, attracting newspaper headlines with its weirder manifestations. The idea of uncontrollable laughter in church seemed to be regarded as particularly eccentric!

I myself was rather uneasy about some of what was happening over that time, and retain some of that unease today. But I remember one evening when I asked for prayer, and found myself gently collapsing onto the floor, where I lay in perfect stillness for the best part of an hour. Members of my congregation were kindly surrounding me and praying for me over that time, but I was hardly aware of their presence. It was the powerful presence of God himself, warming, inspiring, renewing, refining, which took all my attention.

There's a powerful prophecy in the book of Ezekiel where God promises to remove the people's heart of stone and replace it with a heart of flesh; and in many ways I felt that I was on the operating table during that hour, allowing God to deal with my hard-heartedness and to place his strong, passionate heart within me. Eventually I got up from the operating table, hugged those who'd patiently stood by, and made my way back home.

That night I was woken by the telephone at 12.30 a.m. It was someone I barely knew, whose partner had just gone into labour. But tragedy had struck. The baby's heart had stopped beating, and D was about to give birth to a dead child.

Understandably the couple were completely distraught when I reached them twenty minutes later. I too felt totally powerless to anything but stand by their side, weeping with those who weep.

As I pastored that couple through the aftermath of their tragedy, it was a joy to see them turning to Christ and receiving the comfort that only He could bring them. I was delighted to marry the couple and, later, to baptize their children. Somehow that divine encounter had come at just the right moment, freeing me to pastor with genuine compassion in the most ghastly situation imaginable.

Perhaps one more recent story might finish this account. In 2002 I was privileged to visit China in the company of Tony Lambert, an OMF missionary who researches the growth of the church in China. My grandparents were missionaries out there between the wars, and I was keen to retrace their steps, and to witness the burgeoning growth of the church in that great nation.

We spent much of the time in Kunming in Yunnan province, where my grandparents had ministered as doctors, predominantly among the city's many leprosy sufferers – and I was excited to be able to preach at two of the city's house churches, and to find the building where my father was born.

On the last day in China we were back in Beijing, with rather little to do. It was the one rather aimless day in a rich and purposeful trip. Tony and I were wandering round the centre of the city, and a fourteenth-century complex of 'hutongs' (houses built round courtyards), when I asked him whether he knew anyone who lived around there. Yes, he replied, he knew a lady who ran a church from her home.

We went to visit the lady – and I started talking to her mother, who was sitting in the corner of the room, knitting. In conversation I discovered she was ninety-five years old, and had been brought up in Yunnan province. Did she know Kunming? I asked. Yes, she used to work there. Did she know the CMS mission hospital? Yes, that's where she used to work! Rapidly it transpired that she had been my grandfather's deputy between 1935 and 1938!

The statistical chances of such an encounter – sixty-four years after the event, 1,400 miles away from Kunming and in a country with a population of 1.4 billion people – are pretty staggering, but it wasn't the statistics which moved me. Instead the presence and grace of the 'go-between God' who had brought us together was another wonderful foretaste of all that God is preparing for those who love him. For even in these times of encounter we may see as 'in a mirror, darkly'; but then we shall see face to face.

* * *

Michael Wenham *has been vicar of Stanford in the Vale in Oxfordshire since 1989, when he moved from Stockport. The parish is situated in the heart of the Vale of the White Horse and is in many ways typically rural with a large mixed village and two hamlets each with its own church. Michael is*

married to Jane, and they have four children and two grand-
daughters. At the age of fifty-three he was diagnosed with a
degenerative terminal condition. Four years on he continues
in ministry, discovering in the process the Spirit's power to
transform human weakness with love, joy and peace – and
fellowship.

The next morning I was different. I wrote at the time, 'I am
no longer interested in being a good vicar. I just want to tell
people that God loves them'. It might seem an unremarkable,
even long overdue, ambition for someone who had been
ordained in the Church of England for ten years. However, it
felt like a sea change for me.

After a meandering career, I had entered ministry motivated by a sense of mission, sensing that God had equipped
me for it and called me. In my ideals I had pictured myself in
an inner city parish, but in the event had found myself in a
country parish, not far from Oxford. How idyllic! Certainly a
pleasant place, but with people no different from anywhere
else in the planet; assiduous preaching, well-taken weddings,
baptisms and funerals, new ideas for outreach, being nice to
the right people... well, they were appreciated but seemed to
have negligible impact. And so bit by bit, year by year, without noticing it, I began to run dry.

If I was unaware, not everyone was. There were individuals in the church who watched, and prayed for their vicar, for
his spiritual health. As one of them later told me, 'We could
see you were thirsting for something, and we weren't going to
stop until you found it.' Yet this was no concerted campaign
– simply a few who were sufficiently in step with the Holy
Spirit to discern and to pray.

Gradually I woke up to the fact that something was

missing; I began to admit to myself that there were members of 'my' church whose experience of God was more radical than mine and whose lives and eyes showed Christ's love in a way that I could only admire. The problem was that I knew that they would have been considered part of that potentially divisive phenomenon, the charismatic movement, whereas I was water-tight sound with a doctrine that effectively relegated the Spirit to Bible-times and a theoretical place in the mystery of the Trinity. But the disarming factor was that these people were among the staunchest supporters of my ministry and transparently loved me.

I was not too obtuse to realize that there might be a connection between their enthusiasm for the Spirit and what I admired in them. So it was with more than academic interest that I quizzed Jane, my wife, when she returned from a 'quiet day' on the Holy Spirit with a church women's group at the nearby Harnhill healing centre. To be honest I was relieved that, though she had been prayed with, she still seemed quite normal, and in fact had an air of peace. God seemed to know how to cope with my cautious, cerebral nature!

A couple who were involved with overseas development work had returned to the parish, physically and spiritually drained. In their quest for spiritual restoration, David and Anne had spent some months at Kingdom Faith Bible College, at Roffey in Sussex. There, at last, God met them. 'He chooses the strangest places,' I reflected, but there was no doubting the evidence.

Among their friends from that time was a pastor from Burundi, Frédéric, who had been forced to leave by the civil war. He came to stay with them in our village and I remember him one evening in the church, confronting me: 'You know, Michael, the trouble is, you're afraid of God.' And I knew he was right. I was afraid of what people would think of me, but my fear of God was what he might do to me and what he might demand from me. I was frightened of letting him get too close.

At the end of his stay, David and Anne invited us to supper. I don't recall the menu (except that it would have been good), or the conversation, except for one thing which remained with me: 'The king's faith is important for his people'. In other words, my relationship with God matters not only for me, but also for my church. I do recall walking home across the green, enjoying Jane's company and thinking my thoughts. Last thing at night, we customarily pray together for the family and that sort of thing, and that day was no exception. Light out. Settle down. But no. I was far too unsettled. Breaking the precedent of twenty years of marriage, I asked Jane to pray for me.

God answered immediately and dramatically, as it seemed to me. The conversation between my spirit and the Holy Spirit was humbling, yet full of his fiery love. I knew and physically felt that, in spite of everything, God loved me. It was the most liberating and wonderful experience. Jane also felt its physical effect on me, and so was able to answer when I asked a bit later what had been going on, because she too had met that intensity of Jesus' love before we married. God's love enveloped us all night.

So it was not surprising that the next morning I was different. I found myself singing and appreciating songs which I had previously despised as ungrammatical doggerel. The Bible which I had always loved reignited with God's voice. I began to learn not to mind people's disapproval. I discovered a new passion for my wife and an unknown joy in my job.

And I had to rethink my theology – or at least to start to. My conclusion was not that my faith up untill then had been an illusion, or a pretence, but that I had been guilty of resisting or quenching the Holy Spirit. I could not deny that surrendering to him was infinitely preferable, and that where I had been was dangerous ground.

That night, 30 September 1994, opened my eyes to the tangible reality of encounter with God. Whereas I had been able to assert God's activity in retrospect, I now began to find him in the present. It was through one such intervention that I found myself signing up for a part-time course at Roffey Place under the late John McKay, a distinguished Bible teacher, whose mission was to bring together the Word and the Spirit for teachers and readers of the Bible. Under him, I discovered that God wants to speak and act today, not as a rarity, but as the norm. After the last set of lectures on the Gospel of John, I found myself at the foot of Jesus' cross. This was what his love for me meant.

Life is undoubtedly more exciting, knowing this God and in company with the Spirit. It has not, however, become easier. Although I don't feel it, I can understand the perception of others that I have 'flipped', or defected to the other side, and their puzzlement and even discomfort with the effect on my ministry. A few have left the church and worship elsewhere. But, well, this is my story. I can't rewrite it. And it's not finished.

About six years later, I was getting itchy feet. Maybe it was time to move on. Maybe this was a divine discontent moving me at last to that urban challenge I had seen for myself. A vacancy at just such a parish arose. It seemed to fit. I applied, and was short-listed. However, after interview, I had no sense of peace and withdrew – only to be told later I would not have been offered it anyway! Meanwhile all was not quite right physically. I developed what seemed to be a permanently hoarse voice. In the autumn I saw the GP about it, who immediately set investigations in train: ENT consultant, neurology registrar, MRI and CT scans, nerve and electrical tests... It was the National Health Service at its impressive best. And we could guess where it might all be leading.

'Reverend Wenham, would you like to sit down? My colleagues have done all the tests, and having examined them and seen you today, I'm afraid I agree with their conclusion that they all point to your having a motor neurone disorder.' My consultant was direct in confirming my worst-case scenario to Jane and me. But, though it clearly profoundly shocked us, the news seemed to have no power to overwhelm us. Even before we had told anyone outside the family, we had unmistakable signs that God was on the case. A friend from the parish had found an old book, *Briers into Roses*, by Amy Carmichael, written in long-term illness, and heard God telling her to give it to me. The next day a brother came with a miniature rose bush in flower. Four years on it still flowers in the summer.

Now it became obvious why God had not let me move. What my years of proactive ministry had failed to achieve, began to happen. I found myself part of a church which lived out grace. It did not need me, yet it loved me, enough to want to keep me. So now, at considerable cost to themselves, the church members support a weakening and increasingly 'useless' vicar, putting up with my inadequacies, forgiving my mistakes and filling in the holes I leave. They literally weep with me – and laugh too. Their hands are there to support and to embrace us. And they, with many, including ourselves, pray for my healing.

This is not the place to discuss the issues surrounding that. I am not so naïve as to ignore the cast-iron medical prognosis. I can't avoid it as the disease has its way with my body, whittling away at muscle control, gradually paralysing first vocal chords, then legs, and arms. I can't avoid the pain in my wife and children. But I know that all things are possible with God, who raised Jesus from death. Two great consequences follow: the possibility of physical healing and the certainty of an unimaginably better life after death. So, not to ask would be perverse, and not be assured of his perfect answer – whatever it should be – would be arrogant.

In some ways this progressive illness has proved a prolonged encounter with God. It has been a hard but unbelievably rich time. Why he has chosen to meet me like this I no more know than why he chose to bathe me in his amazing love that night six years previously. I have no doubt that the same God who is love is in control and, more than that, has his hand upon my life. And he's still not finished. What's he doing?

First, he's teaching me that the end point of creation was the Sabbath. This fabulously wonderful world was designed to be enjoyed, by God himself, but also by us. Our achieving, acquiring lifestyle excludes us from enjoying this gift in company with its Giver. Now I'm slowed down to Sabbath pace. Secondly, he's showing me how much of a work in progress I really am. Frankly, I'm impressed that he bothers, chipping away at flaws years old. Thirdly, he's been giving me an experience of unconditional, sacrificial love here on earth, and I must say it's awesome, especially as it comes from those who are hurting so much. This is a fresh taste of grace, both sweet and zesty at the same time, and I guess a foretaste of heaven, except that there the hurt will be gone.

We talk with surprising ease of God's love. I have come to conclude that it is infinitely more than we begin to conceive. That love actually includes what I and those around me are facing. All this is done in love, by Love, that love which we humans tried to extinguish on the cross. One day we'll see. Until then we'll hang on, as he did for us in an infinitely darker night.

*   *   *

Betty Craig *was recently widowed after over fifty-eight years of marriage. In 1978, she moved to Shepton Mallet when her husband Alastair retired. They have a large family with six children and many grandchildren. She saw herself as an ordinary mother, grandmother and housewife with little experience other than looking after her home and family. However, contact with the Parish Church of St Peter and St Paul changed all that and took her into new and unknown places.*

When the Spirit Comes!

For me God moves in a mysterious way. As far as I was concerned, he played little or no part in the first fifty-two years of my life, though looking back I now see his hand upon me at various times.

I started life in an incubator in Lewisham Hospital and was baptized by the hospital chaplain when a few days old as I was not expected to live. (As a child I remember being upset because my sister had a godmother and I didn't.)

When I was seven my sister and I went to a new church

school which opened up where we lived, and my mother sent us to Sunday school until we were old enough to object. Part of the time (I can't imagine why!) we were taken into church where the service was that of Matins. After I married, my only connection with the church came through the scout and guide groups to which my children belonged. I became chairman of the church scout group and the complaint that was raised at every meeting was that some of the boys did not turn up to church parade, as they were required to do, and one day I found myself pointing out that neither did we and saying that I proposed to attend the next one.

I suppose something I learned at Matins had rubbed off. When I got into church the following Sunday I knelt down and the only prayer I could think of saying was 'Please let this mean something to me'.

Soon afterwards we moved to Shepton Mallet and, following a visit from the church Road Steward, I decided to go to the church and found myself, for the first time, among a group of people who spoke about God as if he was real. I was invited to take part in a Lent group led by one of the younger members of the congregation. Books were put out in church for us to borrow and I felt compelled to take one home.

I chose the book that I felt would be the easiest to read, largish print, not too long and the only one with a picture on the cover. It was *When the Spirit Comes* by Colin Urquhart, and later, as I read it, I couldn't put it down.

The book told the story of Colin's church near Luton where first one and then other members of the church 'received the spirit'. The following Sunday, having no idea what I was doing, as I knelt at the Communion rail I told God I wanted the Spirit 'like the people in the book'. What was good enough for them, and the apostles, was good enough for me! Not surprisingly, even though I repeated the prayer on two other occasions, nothing happened and I forgot the whole incident.

A few weeks later there was a follow-up day for the Lent groups at Ammerdown (a nearby centre for prayer and conferences); the theme was 'prayer' and again I went home thinking I would pray, something I had never really done before, except formally in church. I sat down, fixed God halfway between myself and the clock on the fireplace, closed my eyes, said 'I know that you are there somewhere', and did my best to think only of God.

After a couple of minutes, I became aware of an odd feeling of happiness, in my body rather than in my mind. It was gentle and pleasant at first but quickly increased and deepened; no longer a puzzling happiness but a joy I felt deep within me – I felt it with my body rather than my mind, right to the tips of my fingers. It was as if it had been poured through the top of my head and nice though it was, I began to wonder what was wrong with me.

And then quite suddenly I knew. I don't know how I knew, but I knew with absolute certainty that it was God. It was as if my whole being knew and the knowledge had come from within me, words dredged up from deep within: 'It is God, oh, it is God'. This moment of knowing came as no shock, but gently with a dawning wonder – released in a fraction of a second which, for me, lives forever, outside time, eternal in itself.

After that, nothing mattered to me, only God mattered, and I knew that the barrier between life and death was very fine, not to be feared at all and easy to pass through. As I sat there, I knew to be dead with God was the same as being alive with him and that I had, in some way, passed through this very fine barrier; and life and death with God had come together.

All this time, the joy had increased and deepened to such an extent as to be almost unbearable. It had become a love such as I could never have imagined possible, a living, consuming love that filled every part of me, moving and alive. It was all around me and in me – it was as if a god from without had come into me and released a god from deep within my soul and the two had come together in an explosion of divine love. The overwhelming feeling was of this love pouring out from me, a living stream, unending, alive yet somehow complete.

And I knew I didn't understand, but that I didn't have to – just to accept.

I tried to capture it in words, the depth of one's soul, the essence of life, the ground of one's being. But I knew I wasn't meant to, and anyway, who can describe God?

Then God said, 'This is my world as it should be for all people' and I knew this to be true. As I sat there I knew myself to be in God's world, at one with him and Creation. God said, 'I have such power in my world – there is nothing I cannot do' and this time I felt his power within me, and I knew the greatness of God.

Again I knew that I didn't understand and I didn't have to, but this time I knew that one day I would, even if I had to die first. Then I knew that God had done all that he intended and that even though I could sit there all afternoon and he would stay with me, I felt that it was impolite to keep him hanging about, so I got up and walked away.

Over the next few months, I continued to experience the welling up of God's love, sometimes with great intensity, at others more gently, but over a much longer period.

Sometimes there were times of guidance, mostly it was the pure joy of walking with God and worshipping him. Eventually I became a reader in the church, something I could never have imagined in my early days.

And so the Spirit came, for me powerful and devastating, yet at the same time gentle; asking nothing, yet irresistible – a divine love that captures the soul and holds it fast in invisible bonds, yet giving it a divine freedom to explore the eternal boundary of its own existence.

Life has taken on a richness and a freedom which still amazes. Nearly thirty years on, I cannot imagine life without God. Yet the question remains. Why me? The only answer I can give is that God moves in a mysterious way.

Janet's Eczema – a Miracle of Healing?

To the family, Janet's eczema had seemed to be forever. It began at a very early age. What was dry, red skin suddenly became a major problem and despite ointments and other treatments she was never clear of the problem. When she was seven, the eczema was so widespread that she was admitted to the children's unit of St John's Hospital for Skin Diseases at Goldie Leigh. This proved to be a long-term treatment; she was there for some four months; we were only allowed to visit at weekends.

Her skin was much improved but it didn't last and she spent two more spells in hospital while she was still at school.

It was distressing to watch and although the family did their best, we could do little to help her, but I don't think we really realized how much her condition affected her until she wrote about it in John Woolmer's book *Healing and Deliverance*:

> Often my clothes would stick to my skin where it was weeping so badly, and my hair would be stuck to my face when I woke up in the morning. The eczema was affecting my life in other ways. I suffered from a lack of confidence due to the reaction I sometimes got from other people. I also found it difficult to join in PE at school or go swimming with my friends. The eczema had taken such a hold on my life that I was increasingly becoming depressed and felt there was no hope for a normal life.

We moved from London to Somerset when Janet was fifteen. At that time I had been suffering from a 'frozen shoulder' for some years. It was very painful and greatly restricted the movement in my arm. John had started healing services in the church and at one of the first of these I went forward for prayer from Don Latham (see page 53). The result was dramatic. As he spoke, I was instantly healed – the pain was gone and I could move my arm freely. It has never returned.

Janet's eczema did not improve with the move and she spent another spell in hospital in Bath with no lasting effect. In her early twenties, with her eczema desperately bad again, and struggling to cope with life, in desperation she asked if she could 'go and see the man who cured my shoulder'. I arranged for her to see John, who prayed with her.

Next day, as she had her usual bath, she called to me to come and see her arm and I can only describe the result as miraculous. The eczema had not just gone from her arm and shoulder, the skin looked normal. John prayed with her regularly over the next few weeks and I watched as the eczema disappeared from one area and then another.

Her life was transformed and that summer Janet was able to go out in a T-shirt and shorts for the first time. Nearly twenty years later, Janet is happily married and almost totally free from eczema, but if ever we see a child with eczema, we both want to weep. She did have one period after the break-up of her first marriage when the eczema returned. She came back for more prayer. This time it again disappeared although much more slowly than on the first occasion.

* * *

Liz Smith *is married to Barry who, apart from running a large firm of opticians, is chairman of the trustees at the Harnhill centre of Christian healing which is near Cirencester. Liz, who was a journalist, now devotes much of her time to counselling. Many people are very grateful for her sensitive listening skills.*

I grew up in a family where God or Jesus were never mentioned. My father was a great reader – particularly of modern history and biographies – but despite his thirst for knowledge, he had no curiosity about religion other than to blame it for being the cause of wars throughout civilization. His credo was to live life to the full without harming others and just get on with it as it was all down to you to make the most of what you had.

I was the second of three girls and as children we were occasionally sent along the road on a Sunday afternoon to the Methodist Sunday school. All I remember is sticking stamps of Jesus in a book and the strong conviction that Mum and Dad just wanted a bit of peace and quiet for an hour or so.

Before I became a Christian, I thought that people who believed in God were smug, self-righteous, narrow-minded and sad. I used to pity them – they seemed mostly unattractive, poorly dressed and boring. They were the kind of people who needed something to cling on to because they had nothing else going for them.

Of course I didn't know any Christians and I'd never even met one! My only brush with religion was an occasional visit to a village evensong with a girlfriend when I was fourteen and the annual Founder's Day service in the local parish church. And while I was surprised and intrigued at what was going on, it seemed to be a rather weird and ancient ritual which had no relevance to my life.

I got married in 1976 and when my second son Rupert was born, my husband suddenly said that he wanted to go to church. At first I was amazed – and then angry. We had never talked about faith and I felt that I had been hoodwinked – the man that I had married now needed something else to make him happy as I obviously wasn't enough. I just didn't understand and the anger tapped into the old feelings that I had had as a child when I felt that the only times when my parents were proud of me were when I did well and passed exams. I had failed as a wife and as a companion, and it left me with a feeling of worthlessness.

My husband's fervour for the faith became intense. It caused many arguments between us because he couldn't understand why I wasn't interested. He joined a Christian businessmen's association and things got a lot worse. He would come home from meetings and tell me how grown men had gone to the front to be prayed for and then had fallen down – overpowered by the Holy Spirit. I thought it was bizarre and unreal. It sounded pathetic that people went along with something that was blatantly untrue and I despised them all for their gullibility.

For the next few years, my husband was a man with a mission – and that mission was to bully, browbeat and bribe me into the kingdom. He left Bible texts casually around for me to see, offered me money to read Christian books, pressurized me into attending family services to 'support' the boys who were now in the Sunday school. I used to look around the congregation and feel that I had nothing in common with these people – I didn't want to be like them and I couldn't say what they were saying because for me it just wasn't true.

But then a series of events happened and things began to change. The church which reluctantly attended acquired a new vicar – a good-looking man who seemed quite normal, but who had an obviously committed belief. Then my husband became depressed and went for prayer counselling at the Harnhill Centre of Christian healing. There he and I met up with the founder, Canon Arthur Dodds and his wife Letty. They were Christians who were fun to be with, compassionate and down to earth. Jesus was a part of their everyday life; they talked to him like a friend – he was the source of their strength and peace.

The following year, my husband suggested going to the airport church at Toronto where there had been a huge outpouring of the Holy Spirit. A holiday sounded nice; but as for the church – I knew that I would have to go along or there would be more arguments.

It was an amazing place – quite scary. I felt uncomfortable and kept looking at my watch, wondering when I could get back to the hotel. The noise was quite frightening – people were screaming and wailing, doubled up on the floor, or crawling around making animal sounds. I was trying not to stare.

There was a call for prayer and after a few tense words; my husband went off into another room to be prayed for. I was aware of the preacher asking for people who wanted to receive the Holy Spirit to come to the front and I found myself getting out of my seat. I had to stand on a line on the carpet with hundreds of others. As the pastor stood in front of me, he held his hand close to my head. I felt an enormous heat on my forehead and fell backwards. I came to when a rather large man fell across my legs and I sat up in a daze. What had happened? I was completely stunned.

God had actually turned up – he had bypassed all my logic, all my reasoning, short-circuited my brain. He had proved his existence by letting me experience the very thing that I had been most cynical about. I knew that I wasn't hysterical or delusional – so God just had to be real.

But while I had been confronted by God's existence, it didn't mean that everything suddenly became clear. There were still many things that I just couldn't make any sense of.

God broke into my life in a spectacular way and over the next few months, I began to change. My old critical attitudes towards those who couldn't get on with their lives, who didn't meet my high standards of perfection, started to fall away. I realized how much I needed Jesus to reach into my heart and restore the damaged emotions that had been ruling my lifelong attitude both to myself and to others. I realized that I found my self worth in being better at things than other people, that getting things right was more important than relationships. I realized that Jesus wanted to show me a way through the past to a place where I felt secure in his love and acceptance – not because I was good at things but because of whom I was as a person – created and loved into being and part of his plan. It was true freedom. I didn't have to be perfect because God wanted me with all my faults, failures and wrong choices. He wanted every part of my life – the things that I was ashamed of, my doubt and disappointments as well as my gifts and attributes.

I now work as a prayer counsellor at Harnhill and in my own church. This has again and again brought me face to face with the God of love, healing, forgiveness and restoration. It is so exciting to see people set free from the burden of pain, shame and guilt that they have been carrying for years and the rejection that they have felt because of physical, emotional or sexual abuse, as well as the despair and hopelessness of feeling unloved and unlovable. I am very privileged to have encountered God working in other people's lives as well as in my own. His grace and mercy is endless, his patience with our rebelliousness unbounded.

In 2001, my eighteen-year-old son Rupert went out for a drink with his elder brother and some friends. We had gone to bed around 1.30 a.m. after a dinner party at home; we were woken by Giles two hours later. Roo had fallen down some stairs and we had to get to the hospital at once.

I don't know how we drove those twenty miles, aching with tiredness, anxiety and dread. Roo was being ventilated; he was unconscious and a brain scan had showed massive damage. He was transferred to a neuroscience unit in Southampton and we followed the ambulance. Surgeons removed several blood clots from Roo's brain. He was heavily sedated and wired up to monitors which measured his pressures and his heartbeat. We drove home in the morning, completely traumatized and in shock. I felt that my whole body had been scoured with some horrible toxic substance –

my heart was burning and thumping with pain, my emotions were reeling in disbelief.

After an agonizing week sitting by his bed, our hopes rising as the pressures dropped and then thrown back into despair as the machines started flashing and bleeping, Roo died. It was the most devastating blow and one a mother never wants to imagine, even in her worst nightmares.

My emotions were in turmoil. My grief was so deep and unrelenting, sometimes I just lay down on the floor and wailed. I felt a huge anger towards God. I felt abandoned and far away from the faith that I had felt so sure about. My husband and I prayed every morning for the protection of our family, naming each one. Yet God just hadn't done it. He had let this terrible event happen – so what was the point of it all? Did he really care or was faith just built on wishful thinking? Was it completely irrelevant when life could deal such a bitter blow?

I knew Roo was with Jesus. But I wanted him here with me. My longing was so intense that it left me breathless. I felt that I wanted to die – not because of hopelessness but because of anger. I wanted to confront that God of love and shout 'Why, why did you let this happen?'

A few weeks later in bed, I cried out to Jesus, 'If you are real, show me. Just get me out of this agonizing place of uncertainty and show me the truth.' Suddenly I had a wonderful picture of Roo with Jesus – they had their arms around each other like mates. Roo was smiling – 'Don't worry about me, Mum,' he said, 'I'm fine.' It was the beginning of my healing.

After much prayer, I stopped blaming God for what had happened. I began to realize that he had been with me through all the trauma and agony. He had never promised to protect me from loss – it was what I did with the loss that was important. I had the sure and firm knowledge that he was right alongside me.

God continued to comfort and reassure me, particularly during times when I was hit by a string of regrets. Had I done my best for Roo when he was growing up? Had I told him how much I loved him? God also helped me deal with the sometimes murderous rage that I felt towards people that I knew had hurt or upset Roo because I knew that I could never make it up to him and make it OK. Only Jesus could do that. Then I had an amazing dream.

I dreamt that I was standing by the kitchen table reading the newspaper when I noticed a pair of feet in sports socks just at the edge of my vision. I looked up and saw Roo – he had this enormous grin on his face and we had a huge hug. It was so real and intense; I woke up, my heart bursting with joy. I knew that the dream was a gift from God. He knew just what I needed. When Roo was in hospital, I couldn't hold him because he had so many lines going into his body. It was something that I was longing to do and God met me right there, where it mattered.

Jesus' promise to bind up my broken heart, release me from darkness and comfort me in my mourning was real. It has been a life-changing experience and one that my family is still working through. I don't understand why Roo died, but I know that my vision for God's purposes is small and limited. When he has worked out his perfect plan, even this senseless tragedy will not be wasted. I know that it has refined me in my work of praying for others and in my relationship with him.

Summary

You have now read the stories of four people whose spiritual lives were drastically changed by their Holy Spirit encounter. For Michael and Liz, the road ahead was particularly challenging. For Liz and Betty, the Holy Spirit encounter was also their conversion experience. For Andrew and Michael, their encounter gave a much needed impetus to their discipleship. Such stories are not unusual. Recently I heard a Catholic monk testify to a similar experience which had opened up a ministry of healing and spiritual direction which he had never previously had.

How can we experience this sort of thing? A good place to start would be to read Luke 13 (especially verses 9–13). The key words are 'ask', 'seek', 'knock' and 'how much more'. We need to ask, we need to be urgent and serious enough to seek and to knock. We also need to understand 'how much more' God the Father wants us to receive. He wants his children to be equipped; he wants these happenings to be normal.

God is sovereign; he will answer our prayers in different ways. For some it may be a gentle quickening of the spiritual current; for others, the swift unblocking of the stagnant ditch. But if we ask, God has promised to meet us (Isaiah 55:6). Our heavenly Father is not a reluctant dispenser of spiritual gifts; he wants to meet us and empower us now and then day by day.

Why not read the key Scriptures (Ephesians 5:18; Romans 8:14–17 and Luke 11:9–13) and then pray? It is usually helpful to pray with other people; they may lay their hands upon you and may also receive some helpful insight as to any spiritual blocks in your life and to how God wants to meet you and use you. Here is a prayer which you could adapt:

Heavenly Father, thank you for the gift of the Holy Spirit which you have promised to all believers. I acknowledge my spiritual dryness and half-heartedness. I long to be filled (anew) with your Holy Spirit and to work only for your praise and glory; please pour out this gift into me. May I experience your love and your power in a new way. May I serve you, and bear fruit for you in your needy world.

Epilogue

[Michael Greed*/Tim Berry]

A S I WAS WRITING THE CONCLUSION of this book, I received this story from my friend Michael Greed who works with the Wycliffe Bible Translators. He helps to supervise the Bible translation work in the Russian Federation.

The Angel of Helsinki

My friend Eric had gone to Helsinki to submit his family's Russian visa applications, but the photos were rejected. They were on the wrong kind of paper. His wife and children were just waking up at our place, over 100 km away. So I whisked them off to the only photo machine I know in Lahti; they had their pictures taken (the ones on the wrong kind of paper were much more flattering) – and I headed off to Helsinki in the car to take them to the Russian consulate. In order to have their visas ready in time for their journey to Russia, for which tickets had already been booked, it was essential that their visa applications were submitted that very day. Time was short. It was now about 10.30, the consulate closed at 12.00, and it was about an hour's drive to the edge of Helsinki. The Russian consulate was right down by the harbour and I had never driven there before. Eric, who was in Helsinki, had my only map!

As I joined the motorway on the edge of Lahti I saw something I'd never seen before – a hitchhiker. So I stopped to pick him up. He was a pleasant, young-ish man, and spoke perfect English. His clothes were pale in colour. I took him to be some kind of nurse since he said he had just been helping someone in Lahti and was on duty in Helsinki at 3 o'clock. As we talked I mentioned that we would be going on holiday in Norway soon, to Mo i Rana and Bodø. He had lived there for a few years.

He was a native of Helsinki. He assured me that he was in no hurry to get to his destination in Helsinki, and since he had a transport pass he could pick up a bus or tram anywhere in the city at no cost. He directed me through all kinds of back streets (when I jumped a red light he reprimanded me), straight through Helsinki, straight to the consulate. All the time he knew exactly which way to go. We arrived in time for Eric. Five minutes after Eric went in they closed the gates to visa applicants.

Without the hitchhiking angel's help and guiding presence, I would never have got there on time. And when we arrived at the consulate he bade me farewell, and vanished. Eric glimpsed him briefly. 'Who was that in the car with you?' 'An angel,' I replied.

Now for the scientific bit. Was he an angel or a person fulfilling an angelic role? I honestly don't know. Either would be possible. What is clear is that Michael understood his hitchhiker, angelic or human, to be a gift from God. All the stories in this book are about God's gifts to us, his people. They are not proofs of his existence; but they are signs of his presence.

To me, as a mathematician, most of these accounts are unlikely to have occurred by sheer chance; in some cases the odds against seem astronomical. This is the hypothesis of the book: God the Creator has chosen to relate to us directly. Consequently, our responsibility is to tell our small part in this great story.

The eloquent apostle of atheism, Professor Richard Dawkins, in his latest book *The God Delusion*, attacks religion in all its forms. I wish that he would take time out to meet and to listen to some of the people who claim to have experienced the living God in so many and varied ways. No individual story constitutes a proof, but the cumulative effect is powerful.

Are all these people deluded? Were the healings and exorcisms just spontaneous remissions; were the dreams and visions self-induced; were the dramatic changes in people's lives a form of self-improvement; was Ian McCormack's death-bed vision a delusion; why did exactly £10,000 just turn up in a collection? Dawkins quotes the philosopher David Hume:[1]

> No testimony is sufficient to establish a miracle, unless the testimony be of such a kind that its falsehood would be more miraculous than the fact which it seeks to establish.

Try that on the encounters quoted in this book. Either my correspondents are grievously mistaken, consummate liars, perhaps both, or they have interpreted their experiences correctly. If the latter is the case, there is a simple explanation. God exists and sometimes chooses to communicate with his creatures in surprising and very clear ways! I know which solution I prefer. I write both as a mathematician and as a spiritual being.

I am amazed and humbled by the way God deals with us,

his wayward children. In the life of Elijah (mainly 1 Kings 17–19) we see many illustrations of this. A widow gives him hospitality and they are fed supernaturally. There is a huge crisis when her son dies and Elijah's desperate prayer is answered. A power encounter on Mount Carmel is followed by depression, an angelic visitation and the still small voice telling him what to do in the future.

I hope that these *Encounters* have breadth and do some justice to the wonderful ways of our God who, despite our many doubts and rebellions, guides and sustains us in the midst of the frailties of life in an increasingly difficult and dangerous world.

In first-century Rome, the leading apostles Peter and Paul were martyred. Before their executions, Mark had travelled with and listened to Peter telling any, who cared to listen, the stories of Jesus; Luke had travelled with Paul carefully recording the adventures of the young church. We are grateful to them that so much of the New Testament is full of wonderful stories (quite a contrast with the Qu'ran, which has none).

Today in our postmodern society, people are largely unpersuaded by, and even uninterested in, intellectual arguments. But they will, pace Dawkins, listen to stories. As I travel around a very ordinary parish in northwest Leicester; I find that people like stories and they are, for the most part, interested in spiritual matters. If we are to get a hearing today, we need to take the 1 Peter 3:15 challenge very seriously and 'be ready to give the reason for the hope that you have' and to speak with 'gentleness and respect'.

What is your story? And before you reply with a diffident shake of the head – just think for a moment how different your life would have been if you had not followed Christ or, alternatively, how different it might become if you now responded to his call.

What a glorious God who, amidst the vast universe, finds time to communicate with his people in such an amazing variety of ways! Wouldn't it be wonderful if each of us, if asked, could share an *Encounter* from our own experience and then help someone else in their personal journey of faith? Each genuine spiritual experience should be like a powerful wave which spreads out and touches many other people.

The poem that brings this book to a conclusion is one such example. Tim Berry was a successful, distinctly agnostic, solicitor when his children dragged him to his parish church. A few months later in 1985, he made a reluctant profession of faith and was confirmed. On Good Friday in 1986, he was given the words and music for this song which became a favourite in my parish.[2] Even the title *Come Follow Me* was remarkable; unknown to Tim, we had just chosen that title for a forthcoming ten-day festival in the church.

> Dark was my life, till the Lord spoke to me
> Hard was my heart and no point could I see;
> Jesus spoke clearly to me, glory be!
> 'Lay down your burdens, come follow me'
>
> Now there's love in my heart for the light of my life,
> Peace in my soul now my Saviour is near,
> Love everlasting and peace evermore
> Oh how I wish I'd listened before.
>
> I know prayers will be answered and all sins forgiven
> Doubts are dispelled and my future is clear

Now I will worship and serve him with joy;
Gladly I'll follow Jesus my King

And so if you're alone and your heart's full of care;
If darkness rules in your life, don't despair.
Seek, look and listen and soon you will see,
He will say clearly, 'Come follow me'!

This was Tim's first significant spiritual encounter. Since then, to his surprise, he has become registrar (the legal advisor) in the dioceses of Bath and Wells and Bristol. He has been able to support several bishops and advise many clergy in difficult situations. His Good Friday *Encounter* is a fine example of what can happen when God intervenes. Isaiah 55:6 says 'Seek the Lord while he may be found; call on him while he is near.' Why not do just that?

Notes

1 Richard Dawkins, *The God Delusion*, Bantam Press, 2006, p. 93
2 The music is available from Shepton Mallet Parish Office, The Bread Room, Church Street, Shepton Mallet, Somerset, BA4 5LE (please enclose a SAE).